The Canal of Panama and Globalization

Andrew R. Thomas

The Canal of Panama and Globalization

Growth and Challenges in the 21st Century

Springer

Andrew R. Thomas
Marketing and International Business
University of Akron
Akron, OH, USA

ISBN 978-3-031-05151-7 ISBN 978-3-031-05152-4 (eBook)
https://doi.org/10.1007/978-3-031-05152-4

This Springer imprint is published by the registered company Springer Nature Switzerland AG
The registered company address is: Gewerbestrasse 11, 6330 Cham, Switzerland

Para Juan Pastor, un gran creyente en Panamá, un
excelente esposo, padre, abuelo, hermano, tío, pollero,
Gatuno, cuñado, y mi buen amigo.

Acknowledgments

This book was many decades in the making. The first time I visited Panamá was 1991. I was awed by everything about the country. Not long after, I married the woman of my dreams who also happened to be a Panamanian! Jackie has been my partner on our great journey together—and my biggest supporter. She has elegantly put up with all my travels to the four corners, especially the last 3 years as this book was finally being written. Our children, Paul Bryan and Alana, have come to see as adults what I saw so long ago: a country whose people passionately celebrate simply being alive as life's greatest blessing.

A book is the result of many people who selflessly give with no promise of reward or riches. My good friend and golf partner Juan Pablo Fábrega gave so much. Without Juan Pablo, the middle part of this book could not have been written. Jorge Luis Quijano was incredibly gracious with his time. Sr. Quijano, it was a great pleasure to tell your story. Panama has been lucky to have you. Manuel Martínez was a wonderful sounding board and listener on our many car trips together. *Gracias, Manuel, por su paciencia y por escucharme*. Robert "Bob" McMillian was instrumental in connecting the dots about the transfer of the Canal from the USA to Panama. Thank you, Bob, for your service to both countries—and the world.

At the University of Akron, Deb Owens has been incredibly supportive of my work over the past 20 years. She is a true light of integrity and a wonderful colleague. My friend Bill Baker is a strong source of counsel and guidance. And, my mentor, Father Dr. Tim Wilkinson always gently points me toward The Way.

Contents

About the Author

Andrew R. Thomas is Associate Professor of Marketing and International Business at the University of Akron and the bestselling author/editor of 25 books.

Some of his works most relevant to this book include:

American Shale Energy and the Global Economy: Business and Geopolitical Implications of the Fracking Revolution (2018, Springer)
Global Supply Chain Security (2016, Springer)
The Customer Trap: How to Avoid the Biggest Mistake in Business (2015, Apress)
The Final Journey of the Saturn V (2012, University of Akron Press)

His book *The Distribution Trap: Keeping Your Innovations from Becoming Commodities* was awarded the Berry-American Marketing Association Prize for the Best Marketing Book of 2010.

Dr. Thomas is founding editor-in-chief of the *Journal of Transportation Security*, contributing editor at *Industry Week*, and, a regularly featured analyst for media outlets around the world such as *BBC, CNBC, Wall Street Journal*, and the *Washington Post*.

Prior to becoming a scholar, Dr. Thomas was a successful global entrepreneur and a principal in the first firm to export motor vehicles from China. He has traveled to and conducted business in 120 countries on all 7 continents.

He shares his time between the USA and Panama.

Chapter 1
Panama, Supply Chain Security, and the Rise of Globalization

Tierra! Tierra! *(Land! Land!)*

—Rodrigo de Triana, the early morning of Friday, October 12, 1492, just off the coast of the Bahamas

Before him spread no paltry lands
To wrest with spoils from savage hands;
But, fresh and fair, an unknown world
Of mighty sea and shore unfurled.

—The American Poet Nora Perry describing Balboa's discovery of the Pacific Ocean on September 29, 1513

The wind is old, but it keeps blowing.

—Roberto Duran, Panamanian world boxing champion and one of the greatest of all time

So everything that ever happened, we knew about in Panama.

—Ruben Blades

In the mind of a fifteenth- or sixteenth-century European explorer, we can be confident that there was a keen awareness of the importance of not only discovering a new trade route but also how secure any new route might be. History tells that Spanish and later other European adventurers traveled to the New World for "gold, glory, and God." Each of those elements certainly played a role in the motives of individual conquistadors such as Cortes and Pizarro and the groups of ambitious entrepreneurs who funded and accompanied them on their wild journeys. While such an understanding has been taught to and recited by school children over the centuries, there is a more proximate and relevant lesson from the European subjugation of the Americas. We would be wise to also consider the vital role that the objective of supply chain security played in making it all happen.

As C.L. Anderson observed, "The finding of America was the greatest event in history; the cruel conquest and almost complete annihilation of its people the greatest wrong known to mankind." Anderson continues, "Human intercommunication and human interrelation were never affected so powerfully as when Columbus, suddenly and within a few years, enlarged the known world by the addition of a new

A. R. Thomas, *The Canal of Panama and Globalization*,
https://doi.org/10.1007/978-3-031-05152-4_1

continent and another great ocean, together comprising about two-fifths of the surface of the globe."[1]

One of the least discussed and understood elements of the rise of globalization over the past 500 years is the role that supply chain security has played in determining outcomes. In today's hyper-connected world, we take so much for granted. We demand that products are transported safely and secure in pristine condition across thousands of miles of oceans, land routes, and the skies. In our ignorance of history, we don't realize how unique the safety and security which we enjoy today truly are: something fifteenth- and sixteenth-century Europeans most certainly understood.

Columbus and the Search for Supply Chain Security

Columbus' journey in 1492 was the culmination of centuries of propositions by earlier scholars that the Atlantic extended to the eastern reaches of Asia. Cosmographers and philosophers such as Aristotle, Seneca, Pliny, Ptolemy, and Solinus believed that the Atlantic was the bridge between Europe and India—and beyond. They also believed the Earth to be round in its shape! In his financing request to the King and Queen of Spain, Columbus liberally quoted the ancients that westward into the Atlantic was *the* best route to India.

While Columbus was promoting his ambition, Europe was facing an existential challenge to its economic power. In 1453, the Ottoman Turks finally conquered Constantinople after centuries of failed attempts. This cut off Europe's control of the overland trade routes to Asia. The security of supply chains between East and West, which had remained robust in the times before Constantinople fell, was now regularly threatened by criminal networks that held up caravans on the passages to the Euphrates and Indus. On the seas, pirate bands swarmed the Mediterranean and Red Sea, hijacking the cargoes of the merchants of Italy.

In twenty-first-century business parlance, the Turkish conquest of Constantinople significantly increased the security risk of the trade routes between Asia and Europe. Controlling Constantinople (modern day Istanbul) for centuries allowed the Europeans to systematically manage the supply chain risks that might be posed to the caravans and ships that moved cargo between the two continents. Of course, in that era like ours, there were pirates, gangs, and other nefarious actors looking to steal and hijack transported goods. Still, the strategic location of Constantinople provided the Europeans with a base of operations from which to effectively interdict the activities of these criminal networks. Traders on both sides of the supply chains were relatively confident that their merchandise—and other valuable transport assets (i.e., people, animals, wagons, ships)—would arrive at their destination safe and sound. This degree of confidence in supply chain security is what underpinned global trade then—as it does now.

[1] Dr. C.L. Anderson *Old Panama and Castillo de Oro* (1911: North River Press, New York) p. xi.

After 1453, European traders and their Asian counterparts lost confidence in the supply chain security that had existed prior. The Turks were not willing to assume the role that Europeans played when using Constantinople's key position to protect the trade routes. Quickly, opportunistic criminal gangs began to disrupt the movement of goods. Hijacking of cargo on the land and the sea became commonplace. And, as a result, the relative stability and security of the supply chains, which had lasted for centuries, fell away. The closing of the East by the Turks forced a growing European population to look ever-more westward for more secure trade routes and, if possible, new markets to trade with.

What, Precisely, Is Supply Chain Security?

The supply chain encompasses all the links connecting a producer to end users. In today's world, links may take the form of production facilities, supplier warehouses, vendor facilities, ports or hubs, retail warehouses or facilities, and outbound shipping centers. Historically, links involve all the ways that goods can be moved by. In earlier times, it was principally the wind as well as human and/or animal-powered transportation. Today, it is a motor vehicle, ship, airplane, or rail car.

A lot can go wrong in the supply chain due to systemic mismanagement and inefficiency, criminal activity, or human error, to name just a few of the threats. That's why the security of the supply chain has always been an important issue for traders, governments, and businesspeople: there's just too much at stake to let problems proliferate or stagnate. It's been estimated, for example, that thieves today steal around $200 billion in goods each year from various points along the supply chain. What's more, problems can grow in magnitude when goods are transported across greater distances and cross-national borders.[2]

Security in its purest form can be defined as the state that is achieved when a stable and safe system exists in which individuals or groups can pursue their ends and objectives without significant disruption or harm and without fear of large loss or injury. Broadly speaking, a security system is designed to keep people from creating problems or hurting other people or property. Security, therefore, is a condition that results from the establishment and maintenance of a system that provides effective protection against violation from hostile acts or influences. Within the security context, there are four elements of the global supply chain:

- The assets (human, physical, and virtual) of the supply chain that must be protected
- Dangerous groups and individuals—both internal and external—who seek to inflict damage and violence on the system

[2] For a more detailed historical analysis on supply chain security, see Andrew R. Thomas & Sebastian Vaduva, Eds. *Global Supply Chain Security* (2016, Springer).

- Inherent vulnerabilities that exist within the system which perpetrators seek to exploit to accomplish their ends
- Security countermeasures that are implemented to protect the system's critical parts through the reduction of risk

As an executive from a global electronics manufacturer that operates in more than 150 countries put it recently, "We can have the most incredible manufacturing and the supply chain dies as soon as it hits the border."[3]

Panama and the Quest for Supply Chain Security

To incentivize the risk-takers who traveled with Columbus on his initial voyage westward across the Atlantic toward what was believed to a secure passage to India, the Crown of Spain set aside a modest annual pension for the first person to spot land. History tells us it was one Rodrigo de Triana who, around 2 a.m. on Friday, October 12, 1492, spotted some distinguishable features on the horizon from his spot on the deck of the *Pinta*. Legend, on the other hand, informs that it was Columbus himself who spotted the coast of the Bahamas a few hours earlier. No surprise that it was the claim of the newly appointed High Admiral of the Ocean Sea, Viceroy, and Governor General of the Indies which won the day. Lowly Rodrigo de Triana was pushed aside. He later returned to Spain penniless and broken: distraught by having fame and fortune robbed from him. After a short while, he left for Africa, where it was rumored Rodrigo converted to Islam, and was never heard of again.

Nearly 21 years later and 1200 miles to the south of where Rodrigo de Triana first spotted land, Vasco Núnez de Balboa and 26 Spaniards under his command became the first White men to wade into the waters of the Pacific Ocean. While Balboa's discovery of the "South Sea" was indeed impressive, a fate even worse than that of Rodrigo de Triana awaited him.

Many historians of the conquest of the New World hold that Balboa's performance in discovering the South Sea is one of its great expeditions. Balboa did not lose a single man in his party during the 4 months he wandered back and forth across Darien: some of the most dangerous territory anywhere on the planet. It is difficult to imagine even in today's world with our modern hygiene and tools that 190 White people could wander on foot across Panama's hostile region of Darien for many weeks without experiencing a single fatality.[4] Nevertheless, within 5 years,

---

[3] Ibid.

[4] Darien remains one of the least accessible places on the planet to human beings. There are still no formal roads nor infrastructure laid in the region. Darien's unapproachability makes it a favorite haunt for smugglers. It is via the corpse-laden footpaths of Darien that thousands of desperate migrants hope to make their way to Panama and then, eventually, north to Mexico and, finally, the United States. Having spoken personally to dozens of these migrants as they emerge from Darien,

Balboa would fall victim to a series of plots and schemes perpetrated by many of the same Spaniards who were with him on that momentous day in 1513. It eventually cost him his head.

So it was: two of the biggest opening acts of the era of human globalization. An era founded on the best and worst of the human condition with contradictions everywhere: high stakes, petty grievances, great ambitions, unbounded jealousies, inhumane behavior, Christ's Gospel of love, wild dreams, brutal nightmares, incredible daring, sensational failure, and unrelenting greed, each accompanied by intrigues too numerous to count.

Columbus returned to the New World three more times after 1492. On his fourth voyage in 1500, Columbus landed on the Isthmus and learned from the natives that there *was* a narrow route between the two seas. A sailor at heart, Columbus clearly and wrongly believed that the locals meant there was a waterway which connected the two seas. Instead, it was a short strip of land which joined the two: Panama.

Despite dozens of subsequent searches of the coasts off the Isthmus by Spanish, Portuguese, and English explorers, no waterway passage across it was ever found. Still, this was not for lack of effort, persistence, nor devotion. The Spanish governor of Panama was sent with orders directly from the King to solve "the secret of the strait" and to accomplish it "at all costs."[5] Like many adventurers, Hernan Cortes, who would later conquer the Aztec Empire in Mexico, came to the New World searching for the illusive strait. Cortes would write to the King of Spain, "If the strait is found… it would make him (the King of Spain) master of so many lands that he might call himself the lord of the whole world."[6]

In the end, Cortes was just half right. In the years after Balboa waded into the South Sea near Darien, other Europeans scoured various regions of the New World for the mythical path between the seas. Jacques Cartier was financed by the King of France to explore what might be a Northwest Passage through the North Atlantic. The ice formations and nasty tides off the coast of Labrador halted his journey there. In 1520, the Portuguese sailor Ferdinand Magellan *did* sail from the Atlantic to the Pacific when he ventured through the treacherous straits at the southern extremity of the continent which still bear his name. However, the short waterway strait between the two oceans that had obsessively preoccupied the minds of Columbus and so many others was never found. It would ultimately take a herculean by the American government in the early twentieth century to finally connect the two great oceans by Canal.

In part, due to Balboa's discovery of the South Sea off the coast of Panama, by 1790, two years after the US Constitution was ratified, Spain still controlled significant portions of the world. The Philippines, territories in Europe and Africa, most of South America, and the vast majority of Central America along with nearly

the harrowing tales of survival while they crossed Darien tell of rotting corpses everywhere along the route.

[5] J. Saxon Mills, *The Panama Canal* (1913, T. Nelson & Sons) p. 3.

[6] Ibid.

two-thirds of the land that make up Canada and the continental USA today were under the Spanish flag. For centuries the sun did not set on the Spanish Empire. Secure supply chains across Panama helped to make that possible.

Panama and the Conquest of the Inca Empire

As the historian Bancroft observes, "Great deeds do not always spring from the greatness of souls".[7] Such was the case for much of the subjugation of the New World by the Europeans. The conquest of Peru and the Inca Empire by Francisco Pizarro, which was launched from Panama, occupies a whole other level of boldness and atrociousness. The story of how Pizarro and a small group of his fellow Spaniards conquered the mighty Incan Empire is one of the most remarkable entrepreneurial adventures of all time. It is also one of the saddest.

Like many young men of his era and class, Pizarro—who was born to the lowest rung of Spanish society and faced a future as bleak as his social standing (his mother left him on the local church steps after giving birth)—desperately wanted to create a new life for himself in the New World. Little is known about this illegitimate, illiterate, day laborer until his arrival Panama in 1509 at the age of 31. After bouncing around for a few years in New Spain, we find Pizarro in 1513 as one of Balboa's lieutenants wading into the South Sea. When the new governor of Panama—Pedro Arias—later asks Pizarro to arrest Balboa on trumped-up charges of fraud in 1518, he dutifully obliges: turning his back on his once good friend. When Balboa is beheaded the following year, Pizarro is standing next to the executioner. For all his loyalty to the governor, Pizarro was awarded the mayoralty of Panama City for the next 4 years. With this new title, wealth and prestige followed. But, Pizarro, who had reached heights beyond anything he could ever imagine as a boy, remained restless. He wanted more. Much more.

In 1524, with rumors circulating in Panama of an empire laden with gold somewhere to the south, Pizarro, along with his partner Diego Almagro, started a company together for the purpose of exploration and the exploitation of this rumored land. The new venture—named "La Empresa del Levante"—was initially financed by Pizarro, Almagro, and Fernando de Luque, the vicar of Panama City. Almagro was an adventurer like Pizarro and a few years older. His illegitimate origin in Spain was as low as Pizarro's. De Luque's high position in the church kept him close to the governor who represented the Spanish Crown's interests and whose blessing was vital for the start-up's potential success.

Also critical to the new venture were other Spaniards who would join the expeditions to provide the manpower and military support necessary to deal with any problems along the way. Like the firm's founders, these fellow travelers were entrepreneurs and incentivized by the promise of a percentage of any fortunes won. They brought with them their own weapons, horses, slaves, and other necessary supplies.

[7] Hubert Howe Bancroft *History of Central America 1530 – 1800* (1886, The History Company) p. 3.

Two separate voyages by the company from Panama over the next 3 years brought Pizarro, Almagro, and their accompanying entrepreneurs into close contact with locals on the coasts of Ecuador and northern Peru. These natives easily traded gold and silver for small, valueless European nick-nacks. They also filled the Spaniards' heads with stories of a nearby inland empire with much more gold and silver. It seemed the company discovered its target market. It then remained to develop an entry strategy.

Upon returning to Panama after this major discovery in 1527, Pizarro decided to head for Spain to meet with the King. Pizarro's logic was that if such an empire of wealth did exist, he would need the complete support of the Crown. He was correct. The King gave Pizarro the appointment of governor, captain general, and mayor of all lands he had discovered or might yet discover. He was given the right to build forts, maintain military forces, grant lands to his fellow Spaniards, and operate with the prerogatives of absolute authority. In exchange for his support, the King ordered that the Crown would receive its "Royal Fifth"—20% of all discoveries and proceeds.

Returning to Panama in January 1530 now with his four brothers, Pizarro met with Almagro and de Luque and plotted what to do next. The following 12 months found them recruiting willing entrepreneurs across New Spain to join them, while raising additional capital to finance the ships and material needed for the job. Interestingly, the Crown provided no financing. All the financial and personal risk was borne by the company. In January 1531, nearly 4 years after their last trip south—and amid great pomp and circumstance across Panama City—Pizarro, his four brothers, 180 other men, 30 horses, and 3 ships finally set off.

As so often is the case—yet remains little understood—is the role that luck plays in the success or failure of a new venture. In this circumstance, the company had certainly planned as well as they could with the limited resources at their disposal. Still, as in every enterprise, uncertainty was omnipresent. Pizarro and his entrepreneurs knew it. What they didn't know—and couldn't have known—were two factors that made their success possible. First was a smallpox pandemic that had been devastating the native populations across Central and South America since the arrival of the Europeans. Second, a bloody civil war had broken out among the Incan elite that was tearing their empire apart. Without these two unforeseen factors at play, it is difficult to imagine that Pizarro and his small band of businessmen could have been successful.

It is not the purpose here to detail further the history of the conquest of the Incan Empire by Pizarro and his band of entrepreneurs—except to illustrate that they were entrepreneurs driven by a tremendous urge to succeed at all costs. The ability of less than 200 Europeans on the far side of the known world to conquer an empire of 12 million inhabitants is an incredible feat for any era. Of course, the suffering unleashed on the locals by the Spaniards in pursuit of their objectives is one of history's greatest tragedies.[8] Suffice it to say, the world was altered inexorably in 1531—and Panama, once again, would be in the middle of it all.

[8] Bancroft's seven volume set about the Spanish colonial period until 1800 known as "The Works" is highly recommend for anyone wanting to learn more about the conquest of Peru.

Roads Across Panama

It is another piece of fortune that the Spanish—among the vast, unexplored expanses of the New World—discovered early on the thinnest thread that connects the two oceans. No shorter route between the Atlantic and Pacific exists than Panama. The Spanish's early and strong commitment to Panama, despite their ignorance of much of the New World, reflects luck as well as their determination and willingness to play whatever cards they were dealt. After Balboa's discovery of the South Sea in 1513—while many explorers pursued the illusive waterway route—others looked for a secure land route across Panama.

What emerged in the period before the conquest of the Incans in 1531 was a transport network across the Isthmus that sought to connect the settlements of Nombre de Dios and Portobelo on the Atlantic side with Panama City on the Pacific. The Spanish colonists were looking to make the movement of people and the transport of goods more reliable and secure between the two oceans. See the map below.

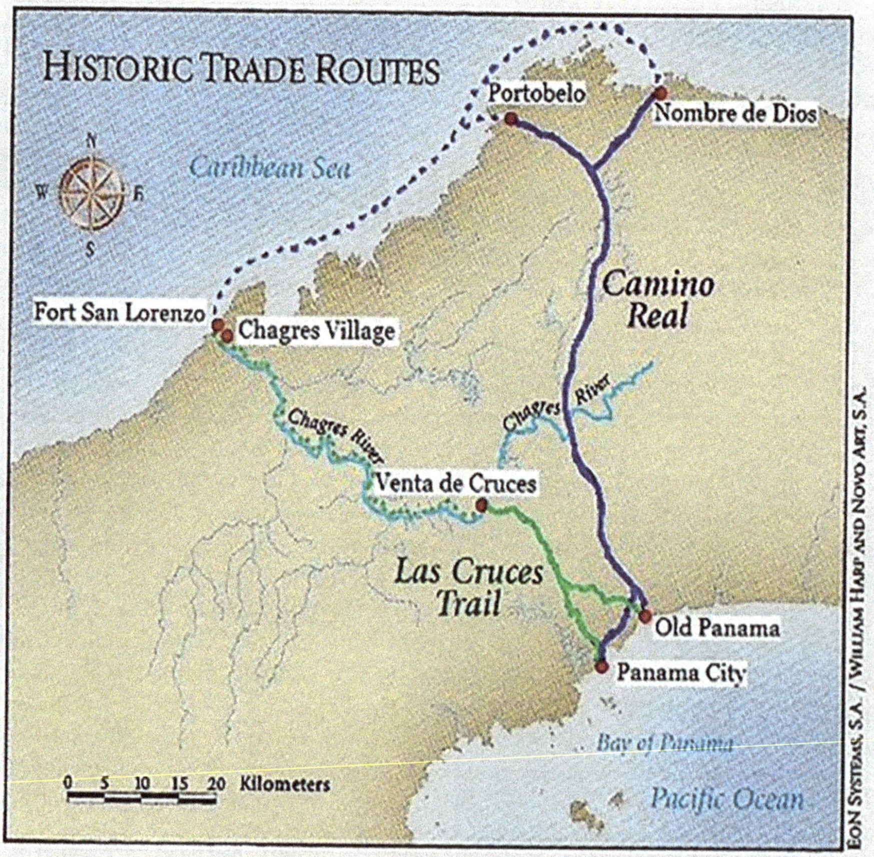

Unlike the Romans, the Spaniards were not road builders. Spend some time today in Latin America, and the lack of high-quality roads across the region is stark. Nevertheless, there was a critical need for secure roads across Panama. Necessity is also the mother of motivation. The first steps took place in the years following Balboa's discovery.[9] Pressing the Spanish authorities, the colonists in Panama were determined to connect the coasts with a predictable, secure transport system. The questions, as always, were as follows: How much would it cost? Who would do the work? And, more important, who would pay for it? These were not easy to answer. No one had ever built a road across Panama before. Doing a cost estimate, therefore, was not going to be easy.

Even more difficult, the highly aggressive natural environment of the Isthmus posed unique challenges, particularly when it came clearing the jungle and wild beasts from any construction site. The geographical position of Panama makes it one of the toughest places on Earth to build and maintain anything. The shortest route between the seas was a deep morass with some of the densest jungle anywhere. It reeked of malaria and was populated by nearly every species of deadly beast, noxious reptile, and venomous insect. Located between 8 and 9 degrees north of the Equator, a sultry, tropical heat, and scorching sun blazed year-round.[10] And, for 8 months each year, torrential rains brought floods, washouts, and the possible destruction of any previous work.

Eventually, an agreement was reached that the costs of the construction would be shared between the Crown and the colonists in Panama. Sometime around 1518, the original road—the "Las Cruces Trail"—was opened. From the south (remember that to move between the oceans in Panama is to move north to south and vice versa), the Las Cruces Trail went as far as the town of Las Cruces and then used the Chagres River to reach the Atlantic by small boat. From there, other vessels would transport people and cargo along the coast to Portobelo and/or Nombre de Dos. The road portion to Las Cruces was paved all the way. It was 8 feet wide and elevated a few feet off the ground.

It was quickly figured out, however, that the security situation was not a favorable one. Once the road/river/coastal network became operational, pirates of the Caribbean started plying their trade and hijacking large amounts of cargo and people on the ocean portion of the journey to Portobelo or Nombre de Dios. Moreover, the rivers provided additional opportunities for pirates to move inland and attack the mule trains at other points along the journey. It was realized another—more secure—route was going to be needed to manage the risk posed by the pirates.

---

[9] As Christopher Ward points out in his seminal *Imperial Panama: Commerce and Conflict in Isthmian America 1550–1800* (1993, University of New Mexico Press), little is written about the roads across Panama themselves.

[10] Fedessenden Nott Otis *Isthmus of Panama: History of the Panama Railroad* (1867, Harper & Brothers) p. 21.

A Quick Detour: Security and Access

At the most basic level, security is about restricting access. This is done by managing the amount of opportunity potential bad actors have to whatever assets we are trying to protect. In the weeks and months after the 9/11 attacks, I was regularly asked in media interviews how we can protect the aviation system from all threats for all time. Such is the shallowness of the modern media today. Anyway, I simply responded that to make sure there are never any successful attacks against commercial aviation ever again, all we need to do is eliminate the human beings from the experience. In other words, allow no one access, including passengers, flight crews, maintenance folks, etc. That way, we could be sure that the security level would be a perfect 100% and no one could cause any harm. Of course, such a possibility is only a theoretical exercise. Airports and planes without any passengers and flight crews are just empty buildings and museum pieces.

In the real world, the best—and only—way to provide the highest level of security possible is to effectively manage the risks posed to the system. That means defining acceptable levels of risk: what can we tolerate and what we can't. The $200 billion annually that is stolen in the modern global supply chain is an acceptable risk for those who use the system. Of course, it would be better if that number was as close to zero as possible. However, to reduce the number of thefts would require the kinds of interventions that could the lower the effectiveness of the system. In cases like these, we make trade-offs. How much are we willing to lose each year to criminal activity in exchange for the benefits of using the system? For those things that are unacceptable, we develop countermeasures to reduce the risk.

In the case of the road network across Panama, to reduce the access of the pirates operating along the coasts and rivers and on land, another road was constructed: "El Camino Real." This route was a single path across Panama that avoided the weak points of the "Las Cruces Trail." Men and mules would walk and ride the 54 miles on "El Camino Real" between the two coasts on a road that was not nearly as accommodating as the 18-mile ground portion of the "Las Cruces." You can still walk portions of both today. Just beware of snakes!

Restricting pirate access—the ultimate objective of the new route—was easier than on the "Las Cruces Trail." Soldiers could be strategically located at points along the way to bolster the security detail of the mule trains: reducing the likelihood of a successful strike by the pirates. Moreover, anyone even suspected of potentially threatening the mule trains along the route was quickly arrested and executed. Sixteenth-century justice being what it was, no investigations were conducted. No trails held.

In many places, "El Camino Real" was only 2–3 feet wide, particularly at a place called "Cuperilla," where drops of 400–500 feet cost the lives of many a man and mule over the centuries.[11] Yet the overall danger to men, mules, and their cargo was

[11]Christopher Ward *Imperial Panama: Commerce and Conflict in Isthmian America 1550–1800* (1993, University of New Mexico Press) p. 48.

offset by the increased security afforded by "El Camino Real" over "Las Cruces Trail." This is not to say, however, that the pirate threat to Panama ever went away. On the contrary, pirates harassed both coasts and the interior of the Isthmus for centuries. For the Spanish, who were always trying to protect their shipments from Peru and across Panama, managing the security risk posed by the pirates remained a top priority in the New World.

While "El Camino Real," despite its longer length, became the preferred route due its higher security level, the less secure "Las Cruces Trail" continued to be used by traders as well. The significant difference in security levels between the two routes was reflected in the comparative cost of transport. From 1547 to 1800, the shorter and less secure "Las Cruces" (18 miles versus the 54 miles of "El Camino Real") still cost on average three times more for mule transportation.[12] Mules were not cheap, and the likelihood of something bad happening was much greater. Thus, despite a much shorter distance on land for the mule trains, the higher security risk on "Las Cruces" resulted in overall higher transport costs.

The Portobelo Trade Fairs: Globalization and Panama

After Pizarro's conquest of the Incas in 1531 and the discovery of vast quantities of gold and silver, the roads across Panama—particularly "El Camino Real"—constituted one of most important commercial routes on the entire globe. For 200 years, the road network became the support structure for the famous Portobelo Trade Fairs. Built upon the model of other European fairs, Portobelo was the hub of the buying and selling of European goods in the New World, as well as the international exchange market for precious metals from Peru.

The Spanish fleet would travel once a year to Portobelo—bringing with it the equivalent of a modern shopping mall. What was sold at the fairs? Wine, oil, wax, books, medicine, lead, iron fittings, iron handles, nails hoes, ploughs, paper, textiles, indigo, cloth, and tobacco seem to have been favorite product categories.[13] Of course, the currency to purchase these goods was primarily the silver—and, also, gold—from Peru. Silver dominated. Over time, the flow of silver from Peru—via the secure supply chains across Panama—resulted in tripling the total amount of silver in circulation in the global economy.[14] An awestruck traveling Englishman in 1637 described the Portobelo Fair he witnessed:

> *...what most I wondered was to the trains of mules which came thither from Panama, laden with wedges of silver, which were unladen in the public market-place, so that there were heaps of silver wedges lay like the heaps of stones in the street... Within ten days the fleet came, consisting of eight galleons and ten merchant ships... It was worth seeing how*

---

[12] Alfredo Castillero Calvo *Economic Tercciaria y Sociedad* (1980, Instituto Nacional de Cultura de Panama) p. 26–29.

[13] Ward, p. 72–73.

[14] Ward, p. 71.

> *merchants sold their commodities, not by the ell or yard, but by the piece and weight, not paying in coined pieces of money, but in wedges which were weighed and taken for commodities. This lasted but fifteen days, whilst the galleons were lading with wedges of silver and nothing else; so for those 15 days, I dare boldly say and avouch, that in the world there is no greater fair than that of Portobelo between the Spanish merchants and those of Peru, Panama and other parts thereabouts.*[15]

With all things, however, nothing is forever. Not long after this account was published in 1648, a perceptible decline began that inexorably led to the end of the famous fairs. In 1668, the pirate Henry Morgan and 460 of his men captured Portobelo and embarked on a 2-week looting and torturing spree. The Spanish government would pay Morgan $250,000 to release the city and its residents from his terror. In 1687, a massive earthquake hit central Peru hard. In retrospect, Spanish Peru never truly recovered from this natural hit. In addition, new routes for the import of consumer products into Peru opened up. Direct shipments from Spain to Peru via Cape Horn and the Magellan Straits replaced the Fairs. Although much longer in distance, the Pacific journey provided more flexibility to buyers and sellers than the once-a-year Fairs. Inventory control and anticipating changes in consumer preferences could be better managed directly rather than through the Fairs. By the early 1700s, the Fairs were shells of their former selves. And, by 1739, a little more 200 years after Pizarro conquered the Incas, the last Portobelo Fair was held. The world, it seemed, had moved on from Panama.

This is not to say that transport across the Isthmus disappeared altogether. The security of the Panama routes was too good to pass up. The British continued to use Panama as the principal route for English goods shipped from Jamaica to Peru and other parts of South America. Silver exports from Peru via Panama to Spain would continue to transit the Isthmus for another century. What went missing was the ability of the Panamanian colonists to partake in the kind of international business that was a cornerstone of the Fairs. With opportunities to trade outside of Panama seriously reduced, the Isthmus fell into a long period of economic stagnation.

As Panama lapsed into a backwater, the nations of Europe still recognized the geographic importance of the Isthmus. Spain built coastal fortifications at a frenzied pace in the second half of the eighteenth century to deter any other Europeans from taking a crack at Panama. Nevertheless, outside of the military and geographic considerations, Panama remained a "has been." To further drive this point home, by the mid-nineteenth century, New Grenada, of which Panama was a part, was on life support. It was a shrinking entity that just a few years before had been the most powerful nation in all Latin America. Now, it was merely a shell of what it had been. By 1831, Venezuela and Ecuador had left to form their own nations. All that remained was an increasingly violent and collapsing Colombia and the remote Isthmus.[16]

---

[15] Thomas Gage *A New Survey of the West Indies* (1648, A. Clark) p. 368.

[16] Originally, the Viceroyalty of New Granada, which was formed by Spain in 1717, was centered in Bogota and included much of northern South America and parts of Central America: the modern nations of Ecuador, Colombia, Venezuela, Panama, portions of northern Peru, and Brazil. Following

Seemingly overnight, however, things changed again for Panama. Eager for diplomatic recognition from the rising United States, New Granada in 1846 gave the American government permission to construct a railroad or a canal across the Isthmus, so long as passage for anyone wanting to use it remained open. The "Yankee Strip"—as it came to be known—was a piece of land approximately 10 miles wide and 50 miles long that assured American sovereignty over it for at least the next 50 years.

As the Railroad in the nineteenth century and the Canal in the twentieth century became the dominant routes across the Isthmus, Panama's importance to the global supply chain network steadily increased once again. This time, it would be the ascendancy of the United States, not Spain, that would link Panama to the heart of globalization.

The Railroad Between the Seas

It is not hyperbole to observe the building of the Panama Railroad as one of humankind's most incredible engineering successes. As Dr. Otis presciently observed at the time, "In ancient or in modern times there has, perhaps, been no one work which in a few brief years has accomplished so much, and which promises for the future so great benefit to the commercial interests of the world."[17] Among the many tremendous outcomes of being able to travel securely from ocean to ocean in a couple of hours, the achievement of laying the tracks across Panama turned the centuries-long dream of a waterway across the Isthmus into a distinct possibility. It was the Railroad's completion in the early 1850s which later convinced President Theodore Roosevelt and the American government that construction of a Canal across Panama was finally feasible.

While volumes have been written about the building of the Canal, little is known about the Railroad's construction. Only a few books and articles have explored the Railroad's massive undertaking; and, many gaps in this compelling narrative remain wide open. For example, as the Railroad was privately financed, what was it in the character of the venture capitalists, engineers, and workers who risked so much to make this possible? What drove them to put their own money, reputations, and lives on the line toward an enterprise that to so many looked so foolhardy? Where did men like William H. Aspinwall—the lead investor—and George Totten, the chief

---

the expulsion of Spain from the New World in the 1820s, the Viceroyalty was dissolved. The newly liberated peoples created Gran Colombia; and, for a few short years, it was the most powerful country in Latin America. Nevertheless, an inability to stay unified led to fracture, with the areas of Venezuela and Ecuador breaking off in 183. The end of Gran Colombia quickly followed. The Isthmus, which remained under control from Bogota, was rolled into a slimmed-down version of the original New Granada, where it stayed until Panama's independence in 1903.

[17] Dr. F.N. Otis, M.D. *Isthmus of Panama: History of the Panama Railroad* (Harper Brothers, New York) p. 15.

engineer, find the fortitude to carry on when all seemed lost? We will never know. They left behind little valuable correspondence that could provide such insight.

What we do know is that they were driven as so many entrepreneurs are by the belief that they would be able to achieve a strong return on their investment of time, capital, and risk. Moreover, luck—as in all human endeavors—played a significant role in getting the Railroad finished. Whether we call it randomness, variability, unpredictability, or something else, luck plays a far greater role in life than we usually recognize. And, that was the case in completing the Panama Railroad.

Opportunities Not Seen

During the first phase of the Railroad's construction, the California Gold Rush got in full swing. Thousands of eager gold seekers from across the Eastern United States scrambled each month to get to New Orleans, New York, and other ports to book an Atlantic passage on a steamer to Panama. The 49ers entered the Isthmus at the mouth of the Chagres River and then proceeded 60 miles across Panama via a transport mix of native canoes, donkeys, and their own two feet. The trip averaged 5 days: 10–12 miles per day. The boat trip up the Chagres took about 3 days. The last two were spent crossing the Continental Divide on a wretched trail of 20 miles.[18] Once in Panama City, the 49ers battled for a ticket on a ship to make the Pacific journey to San Francisco.

Interestingly, while thousands of well-heeled Americans burning with gold fever each month were desperately trying to get across Panama as fast as possible, the Railroad never entertained the idea of transporting them. The original docks for the railroad were constructed on Manzanillo Island near Navy Bay (which is now the city of Colon) to receive the building materials from New York and the laborers from Jamaica and Cartagena. Even more, George Law, the Director of the Panama Freight Line, whose ships transported the 49ers to Panama, was also a large shareholder in the Panama Railroad Company. Like the other Railroad directors, Law simply never considered using the uncompleted Railroad to move passengers. The distance between Manzanillo Island, where the Railroad started, and the mouth of the Chagres River, which was the disembarkation point for the crazed 49ers, is about 12 miles as the crow flies. It could have been a thousand. See the map below.

[18] Joseph L. Schott *Rails Across Panama* (1967, Bobbs-Merrill Co.) p. 47.

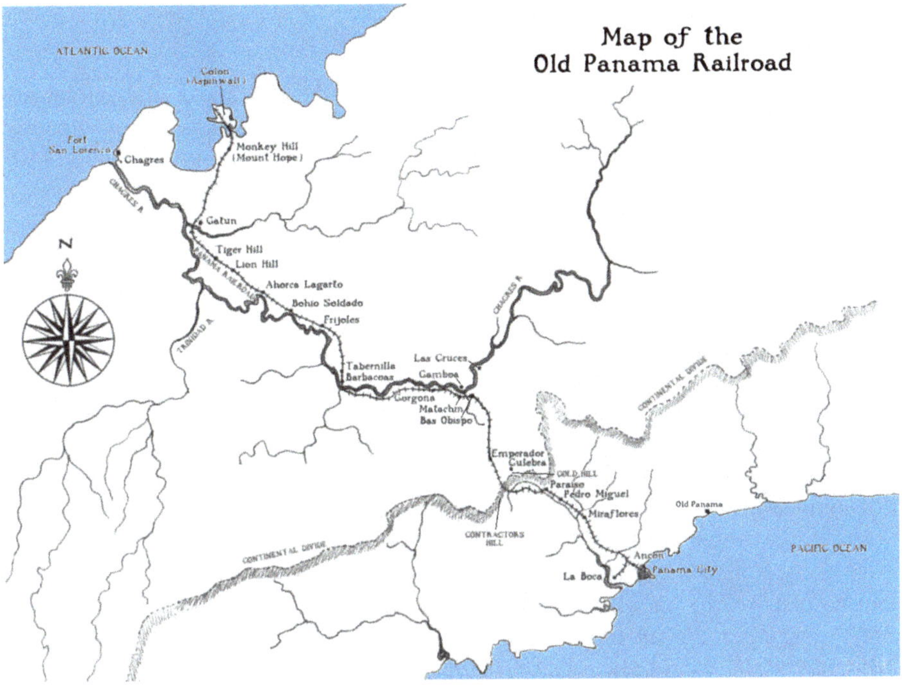

On the Verge of Collapse

By mid-1851, the Railroad project was falling apart. Delays, cost overruns, the horrible tropical weather, disease, chronic labor shortages, and much more had brought things to the edge of failure. The value of the Railroad's stock had fallen to almost nothing, and, no one seemed interested in ponying up more capital to keep things moving. Yet, on October 1, a train of working cars, drawn by a locomotive, finally reached Gatun, 8 miles from the head of the Atlantic terminus. While this was viewed as a great success by the engineers and the workers on the ground, the investment community was unimpressed. It had taken 20 months and a staggering $1 million to go just 8 miles. For reference, the initial projection of the completed construction of the entire 50-mile long Railroad was $3 million within 36 months.

Speculation was gaining that the Railroad might just simply end at Gatun some 40-plus miles short of its goal. The flow of construction materials diminished to a trickle and then dried up. The workforce was reduced to a few engaged only in critical maintenance trying to protect the partially completed line from the onslaught of the rains, floods, and the tropical jungle. By late November 1851, the Panama Railroad Company was on the verge of bankruptcy.

A Flash of Light

Then, one of those "moments" happened that changed the course of global transport and international business. Sometime in mid-December, two large steamships, the *Georgia* and the *Philadelphia*, arrived at the mouth of the Chagres with around 1100 passengers *en route* for California via the traditional river/land passage. However, the weather was so ferocious that, after several lives had been lost in trying to make a landing, the ships were forced to seek refuge in the harbor of Navy Bay.

While waiting for the seas to calm, the unmistakable sound of a locomotive's horn roused the frustrated passengers. It was the daily work train carrying laborers and materials up the line. Then, someone lost to history came up with the idea that instead of waiting for the weather to improve in order to return to the Chagres and begin the river route, why don't the passengers simply jump on the working cars of the railroad and travel the 8 miles to Gatun? From there, they could pick up the regular journey to the Pacific.[19] As word of the idea spread, it was clear the 49ers were not going to be deterred. A delegation was eventually sent by the passengers to meet with George Totten, the Railroad's chief engineer.

Initially, Totten was against the idea. Passenger cars were never sent to Panama—and no discussions on what to charge prospective riders were ever held. Further, Totten had no authority to negotiate such a deal. Still, on that day in December 1851, the 49ers would not relent. They claimed they would pay whatever Totten asked. Wanting to calm the situation and discourage anyone from potentially hijacking a train, he quoted an exorbitant fare of 50 cents each mile, plus 3 dollars per 100 pounds of luggage. To Totten's amazement, nearly all the 1100 passengers happily paid the asking price and scrambled onto the work cars. By the day's end, each of the passengers had been transported safely to Gatun, and Totten had collected for the Railroad almost $7000 in US currency![20]

Fortunes changed immediately. All future passengers bound for the Pacific on Law's steamers would now be unloaded at Manzanillo Island, not at the mouth of Chagres. The Railroad rushed passenger cars to Panama. When, a few weeks later, the company released a new stock offering of $4 million in New York, it sold out within hours. More stock offerings came later and enthusiasm for each of them was equally high. The trains now met every steamer as it arrived—and the 8 miles of track from Manzanillo Island to Gatun became the most profitable trip anywhere in the world.

It almost goes without saying that the Panama Railroad Company had nearly missed a tremendous opportunity to save itself and unknowingly change the fortunes of the world. Had the Railroad gone bankrupt, we may have never seen the building of the Panama Canal. Even when faced with blinding tunnel vision, luck can and does play its part.

[19] Schott., p. 32.

[20] Schott, p. 102.

Securing the Way for the 49ers

The sudden rush across Panama by the 49ers to the Pacific, in conjunction with the final completion of the Railroad, ushered in a new era in the history of Panamanian and global transport. Prior to crossing the Isthmus on the Railroad became available, the old trails of "Las Cruces" and "El Camino Real" were born again, as well-heeled Americans heading to California to strike it rich saw Panama as the quickest route to the West Coast. The trails had fallen into significant disrepair over the years. Notwithstanding the many challenges this posed to travelers, the "gold fever" that had struck so many made them almost oblivious to whatever obstacles were in front of them. They were going to California come hell or high water.

With these developments also arrived a new breed of criminal on the Isthmus. It was open season for them. The Yankee Strip had no law enforcement officers or government officials on it. There were simply no laws. It was everyman for himself. Everyone carried their own guns to look out for his life and property, yet if they lost both, nothing official was ever done about it.[21]

To better manage the risk of moving large amounts of people, cargo, and, increasingly, gold discovered in California that was being sent back East, several express companies were established in Panama to facilitate and secure transport. The express companies would organize mule trains across the Isthmus for their customers and provide armed guards along the way. A name from this era we might recognize today includes Wells Fargo. Upon arriving in Panama City in 1849, their agent, Henry Tracy, did not like what he saw of the security situation. He wrote to his boss, "There will have to be bloodshed before matters become regulated. I have no doubt within 6 months there will be an attempt to seize one of the large, but half guarded mule trains."[22] In August 1850, the first important robbery occurred, when a pack train on the Cruces Trail was attacked by masked men who made off with $30,000 into the jungle. This turned out to be a small heist compared to what came later. Over the next year, more brazen attacks would follow. Murders became more and more common. The biggest single attack occurred in September 1851 when a gang attacked a pack train near Gorgona on the Cruces Trail, stealing $250,000 in gold and killing several express company guards.

Following this attack, William Nelson, the US Consul at Panama City, and also a partner in an express firm wrote in a letter to William Aspinwall that local criminal bands are now being re-enforced by the influx of hardened criminals from all around the world. He warned that something drastic must be done "to curb these criminal excesses, or all Isthmus freight routes will be imperiled."[23] Over the next few years, under tremendous pressure from the Railroad and the express companies, American and Panamanian officials began working together to conduct a systematic purge of any known criminals. Unlike the Spaniards, who willfully executed pirates that

---

[21] Schott, p. 60.

[22] Ibid.

[23] Schott, p. 61.

threatened or molested travel across the Isthmus, criminals caught in the early 1850s were either imprisoned in Panama or sent back to their home country for punishment there. Ultimately, the pressure of consistent law enforcement across the Isthmus provided a strong deterrent to the activity of criminal networks there.

The Success of the Railroad Finally Makes the Canal a Reality

The motives for moving beyond the Railroad to a Canal as the principal route between the seas were obvious: greater efficiency, security, and, ultimately, lower costs. Cargo and people could be more easily transported via ship across the Isthmus than even by the Railroad. There were far less touchpoints on a journey, say, from Southampton United Kingdom to San Francisco via a Canal (ship) than the Railroad. The fewer the touchpoints on the supply chain, the lower level of access and, therefore, less risk of something going wrong. Cargo and/or passengers could be loaded in England in a self-contained vehicle (a transoceanic vessel), sail across the Atlantic in that same vehicle, enter the Canal, navigate the journey across Panama, and continue onward to San Francisco—safe, secure, and predictable.

The Railroad journey involved disembarking cargo and/or passengers on the Atlantic side (a touchpoint), boarding the Railroad (another touchpoint), and crossing to the Pacific side to find a new ship (a further touchpoint or two). Each of these touchpoints presented the opportunity for increased access and risk: particularly delays and thefts from multiple cargo handlings. Each of these elements raised costs and risk.

Of course, the Panama Railroad was certainly a huge step forward in providing a more secure route between the seas than the old road network. During the first 13 years of the Railroad's full operation, more than 400,000 passengers were transported across the Isthmus via the Railroad, and it was not known of a single case of sickness which had occurred as a direct result of the transit. The amount of currency or its equivalent in precious metals moved was $750 million, without the loss of a single dollar. Moreover, 300,000 bags of mail were transported, none of which went missing—all this in addition to the tens of thousands of tons of freight that moved nearly unscathed across Panama.[24]

Success has many children. It would not be a stretch to say that the Railroad spawned the Canal. As the Railroad continued to generate strong profits and returns for investors in the decades after it opened (an average return of 15% a year until 1890), its fortunes were closely observed by those with ambitions to finally build a Canal across Panama.

[24] Otis, p. 49.

It is not the purpose here to recount the American effort to complete what the French started. Dozens of books have already well-documented the awesome engineering feat that was the building of the Canal by the United States.[25] It is truly one of humankind's greatest accomplishments. Suffice it to say, the Americans picked up the ball where the French dropped it and were able to successfully get across the finish line. Building the Canal was the culmination of a four-centuries dream of a completely secure supply chain between the two principal oceans of the world. Once large ships carrying cargo and passengers could quickly and safely traverse Panama, the true benefits of supply chain security were realized.

[25] I am regularly asked to recommend books to general readers about the building of the Canal. Two stand out in my mind: David McCullough's *The Path Between Seas: The Creation of the Panama Canal 1870–1914* (1977; Simon & Schuster) should be the starting point for anyone looking to learn about the Canal. Also, J. Saxon Mill's *The Panama Canal* (1913) provides a contemporary look at the construction of the Canal as it was unfolding.

Chapter 2
The Canal and American Ascendancy

God has a special providence for fools, drunkards, and the United States.

—Otto Von Bismarck

Why don't we get out of Panama gracefully, before we are kicked out?

—President Harry Truman, 1947

The world moves, and ideas that were good once are not always good.

—President Dwight D. Eisenhower, 1956

Been there. Done that. Got the T-shirt.

—Popular American Saying

The audience at the presentation of the John Fritz Gold Medal on March 23, 1925, in New York constituted some of the greatest minds of the day. Thomas Edison, a previous winner of the award, was there. So was J. Waldo Smith, the engineer who designed New York City's water supply. The inventor of the wireless telegraph, Guglielmo Marconi, was seated in the second row. Orville Wright, who had lost his brother 12 years earlier and yet continued to persevere as an innovator, traveled from Ohio to join the crowd. As did Sir Robert Hadfield, the inventor of manganese steel, who sailed from London.

They sat among other dignitaries from Wall Street, the US Congress, and high-ranking representatives from the Russian, French, Japanese, and Chinese governments. The gathering was to honor John F. Stevens, a man whose life was nearly an embodiment of the nation he came from. For in the time that Stevens was alive, America rose to heights that have been unparalleled in human history.

He was born on a small farm in 1853 and died at the age of 90. John Stevens was a member of the generation that saw the destruction of the Civil War as a child and the reconstitution of the nation as a young adult. He lived nearly all his life at the front, literally blasting and bridging his way across the United States, Panama, and the world. In his later years, Stevens would help drive a rising superpower onto the world stage.

He was self-made thru and thru. His philosophy was simple and uniquely American: anything can be accomplished by hard work. He believed in what

A. R. Thomas, *The Canal of Panama and Globalization*,
https://doi.org/10.1007/978-3-031-05152-4_2

ordinary men could do if they just did it. He often said that hard work was the only "open sesame" he knew of.

He learned surveying at an early age. It allowed him to move up the ladder—albeit the hard way—in the burgeoning railroad industry. He was first a track hand in Texas and then a junior engineer, locating and building railroads in New Mexico, Minnesota, and British Colombia. In 1886, he was given the herculean task of building nearly 400 miles of line through the swamp and pine forests of Michigan's Upper Peninsula, from Duluth to Sault Ste. Marie. He did it. After all, it was only work. Three years later, James J. Hill, the bigger-than-life President of the Great Northern Railroad, made Stevens one of his top engineers. Hill was looking to build a railroad from Havre, Montana, to the Pacific. It was to be Hill's personal road to empire.

The story that most railroaders know of Stevens occurred in the dead of winter in 1889. Navigating the snow-swept Rockies alone after his Indian guide had abandoned him, Stevens discovered Marias Pass. He was on foot and it was getting dark. Without wood for a fire and the temperature plummeting to 40 degrees below 0, Stevens walked through the snow in the same circle all night so as not to freeze to death. The next day he returned to the base camp where he informed Hill of the discovery, which would save his railroad 100 miles through the Rockies. Even more important, the discovery of Marias Pass allowed for the opening of America's Glacier National Park.

In 1895, Hill made Stevens his chief engineer and, ultimately, his general manager. Stevens constructed bridges and tunnels and, by the time he was 42, had built more than 3000 miles of railroad, more than any other man in the world. The track he laid was in some of the most foreboding places on Earth. Through it all, Stevens survived Mexican fevers, Indian attacks, Upper Michigan mosquitoes, and Canadian blizzards. Raised on the Frontier, he exuded the restlessness of his times. Even while taking on a new assignment, he always seemed to be thinking about the next.

It is not part of the conventional wisdom that the US effort to build the Panama Canal nearly fell flat on its face. Yet, in fact, the first years of the effort—1903 and 1904—were marked by tragedy, fear, and panic. By 1905, it was becoming clear that things were on the road towards disaster. Something drastic needed to be done. Theodore Roosevelt—"the Empire Builder"—whose credibility and presidency were on the line called for new leadership of the project. It was John Stevens, Roosevelt was told by James J. Hill, that would save the day. Hill told the President it was only Stevens who could overcome the yellow fever, landslides, torrential rains, and chaos that had come to symbolize the American effort at Panama.

Quiet and unassuming, sure and unhesitating, Stevens accepted the President's offer and within 2 years had saved the American effort and "made the dirt fly." Colonel William Goethals, the chief engineer who oversaw the completion of the Canal and whose own work at Panama is heralded by a cascading waterfall at the base of the Administration Building, says of Stevens: "The Canal is *his* monument."

After Panama, at a time in life when most men who had achieved his level of success would have retired, Stevens sat among the tombs of the ancient Manchu dynasty, amid the conflicting storms in the two great historic civilizations of Russia and China, casting his eyes still farther westward, across the reaches of Siberia to the Ural Mountains.

In May 1917, President Woodrow Wilson asked Stevens to go to Russia to head up the American Railway Advisory Commission and study how to improve the Trans-Siberian and Chinese Eastern Railways, an essential factor in preserving Russia as one of the Allies in the Great War. Stevens was subsequently appointed advisor to the Russian government under the Kerensky regime and then by the Chinese government as Administrator of the Chinese Eastern Railway.

During these days, it must have been remarkable to witness Stevens' office, as throngs of Manchurian leaders, Japanese diplomats, civilians, and bureaucrats, Cossacks, Frenchmen, Englishmen, Chinese generals, and Americans of all kinds, united by only their faith in one man, who seemed to be the sole disinterested factor in that bewildering situation, poured in.

Because of these great accomplishments—and many others—Stevens was awarded the Distinguished Service Medal from the United States, Officer of the Legion of Honor of France, Second Class Order of the Rising Sun from Japan, and the Order of Wen Hu, China's highest military decoration. He was bestowed honorary degrees from the University of Michigan, Bates College, and the University of North Carolina.

Stevens especially cherished the John Fritz Medal. It came from his peers: the civil engineers who built so much of the country he loved so dearly. His words of acceptance that night in New York echoed Stevens' respect for his chosen profession and the life he lived:

> *It is now more than a half-century, fifty-fours years to be exact, since I, as a raw lad, without money, influential friends or technical training (I had never heard the last expression), cast my hat into the ring and decided upon an engineering career. Just why I did so I do not know, for other than perhaps a natural aptitude for higher mathematics and a very decided tendency toward wanderlust.*
>
> *Many times during that long period when a fairly successful career looked so uncertain, I asked myself: "Is it worthwhile? Why not just drift along as so many are doing, for the result will be the same in the end?"*
>
> *But I think I was fortunate in that for years my work took me away from the petty trumpetry of civilization into the wide-open spaces and among the mountains, where one lives close to Nature, who is the great Comforter and Mother of us all and who is ever ready to whisper a word of cheer to the despondent.*[1]

To understand the life and contribution of John Stevens is to gain new insight into the coming of age of the United States and America's Ascendancy. From the ashes of the Civil War, a new, unified country filled with vast natural resources and brimming with all the elements of greatness began to emerge. From the closing of the Frontier to the building of the Panama Canal to the rise of the Nation as a global

[1] The details of the presentation of the John Fritz Gold Medal, including Stevens' comments, that occurred on March 23, 1925, as well as the list of attendees and other particulars are contained in the official program, which was published by *The De-Vine Press* for the American Society of Civil Engineers.

superpower during and after the World Wars, Stevens was right in the middle of it all. And he, like his country, moved mountains.

To get a deeper sense of the role the Canal has played—and will play—within the global capitalist system, it is vital to understand its connection to America's Ascendancy. They are quite related. Metaphorically, the Canal is a cousin to the twins of America's rise and the international system it created and has maintained since 1944.

I realize the above paragraph needs to be unwrapped. There is a lot there. First is regarding the Canal. In this context, the Canal is held as a component, an element, a piece, or the like that has contributed to the inexorable rise of the United States and globalization. The Canal is part of a collection of assets that has fueled—and continues to fuel—America's singular position in the world and the global economy it underwrites.

Second, the rise of the United States has been the biggest story for much of the last 150 years. While other nations have risen and fallen, it is the United States that has alone achieved the level of a truly global superpower. As Michael Beckley puts it so well:

> *...in terms of wealth and military capabilities- the pillars of global power- the United States is in a league of its own. With only 5 percent of the world's population, the United States accounts for 25 percent of global wealth, 35 percent of world innovation, and 40 percent of global military spending. It is home to nearly 600 of the world's most profitable corporations and 50 of the top 100 universities. And, it is the only country that can fight major wars beyond its home region and strike targets anywhere on Earth within an hour, with 587 bases scattered across 42 countries and a navy and air force stronger than the next 10 countries combined.*[2]

The esteemed Yale historian Paul Kennedy further points out, "Nothing has ever existed like this disparity of power; nothing." The United States is quite simply "the greatest superpower ever."[3]

The Canal as Auxiliary to American Ascendancy

The United States built and operated the Canal exclusively until 1979 and then shared operations with Panama until the handover in 2000.The purpose of the remainder of this chapter is to put the Canal in its proper context when it comes to the rise of the United States—and globalization. It is complicated and requires a penetrating look at several areas that seemingly lie outside of the Canal. I ask you, the reader, for patience as I seek to weave everything together.

What follows might be a tough pill to swallow for some. Yet, it still needs to be stated: much of the time that the Canal was under American control, it did not create a whole lot of value for the United States. At moments, it seemed like a burden.

[2] Michael Beckley *Unrivaled: Why America Will Remain the World's Sole Superpower* (2018, Cornell University Press) p. 1.

[3] Ibid.

Eventually, owning and operating the Canal became a liability. The continued devolution of the Canal's value to the United States would in due course find the Americans cutting it loose.

Now, of course, the Canal *did* make valuable contributions to the United States at one time or another. Particularly in the early days after it opened, the Canal helped to facilitate America's continued economic expansion westward across the continent. The rise of cities like Houston and Los Angeles had much of their early success due to the Canal. Nevertheless, as Harry Truman and Dwight Eisenhower each observed about the Canal, ideas that once seemed good ones often become not so good. From an American perspective, this was the case of the Canal. The Americans built it, paid for it, operated it, and assumed all the risks associated with each undertaking. Over time, it simply wasn't worth it to continue. The rewards weren't there anymore.

A Prescient View of the Canal in 1914

As the Canal began limited operations in 1914, an obscure German academic, Dr. F. Zadow, wrote an article looking at what the Canal meant for the future. Like others before him, Zadow correctly identified that the political importance of the Canal was greater than its economic value. It was not built by the Americans principally as a trade route but as an instrument of war.[4] President Theodore Roosevelt used the military argument when he lobbied Congress to build the Canal in the first place. Roosevelt sold Congress on the notion that the Canal would allow the US Navy to move between the Atlantic and Pacific in a matter of a few hours rather than the several weeks needed via the Straits of Magellan. In his analysis, Roosevelt justified the massive expenditures required to build the Canal by arguing that America would never require a second battle fleet.[5] Just one fleet plus the Canal would do the jobs of protecting both of America's coasts and quickly projecting naval power wherever needed.

Zadow saw the Canal much differently. He predicted that it would quickly increase tensions between the United States and Japan. He saw the building of the Canal as a serious setback for Japan. Zadow observed that the Philippines, which had served as a key base for the US Navy since their seizure from Spain in 1898, was no longer crucial. Instead, the Canal allowed the Americans to fully exploit Hawaii as their base of naval operations. "The possession of the Hawaii Islands is equivalent to the mastery of the Pacific," Zadow wrote. He then continued: "The United States is now establishing on the island of Oahu a fleet-base (Pearl Harbor)

[4] Dr. F. Zadow "A German View of the Strategic Importance of the Panama Canal" *U.S. Naval Institute Proceedings* Volume 3, 1914, p. 803.

[5] The final cost of the Canal was around $350 million by 1914, which is over $8 billion in 2022 Dollars. This may seem like a reasonable amount through the lens of today—where trillions have replaced billions when it comes to government spending. In 1914, however, the entire outlays by the Federal Government that year totaled $725 million!

of extraordinary strength and importance; the first blow of Japan would apparently fall on this base."[6] He concluded with "It is seen that the Panama Canal will soon be the cause of a tremendous conflict." Twenty-seven years later, the Japanese attack at Pearl Harbor proved him right.

World War II and the Canal

Paradoxically, World War II would ultimately reduce the Canal to an auxiliary status of both the US Navy and America's global ambitions. As Dr. Zadow observed, the series of events unleashed by the building of the Canal led—in part—to America's entry into the conflict. Noel Maurer and Carlos Yu in their compelling book *The Big Ditch* took a deep, empirical dive into what benefits the United States derived from the Canal during World War II. Maurer and Yu found that the Canal's impact on the American ability to wage a successful two-front war was minimal. They concluded, "The naval might of imperial Japan would have been overwhelmed by American industry, with or without the Panama Canal."[7]

The war also fully introduced the aircraft carrier as the most effective and quickly available military instrument of national prestige.[8] During and after the war, the Americans embarked on a massive building program of aircraft carriers. Like today, aircraft carriers were viewed as vehicles of the most widely diverse capabilities, "the bridge between the traditional and ultramodern instruments of military power."[9] As carriers got bigger and bigger, the Canal simply could not handle them. The locks were too small.

By the 1950s, driven by the strategic goal of deploying more and more carrier groups, America had developed a multi-ocean fleet navy: the opposite of what Teddy Roosevelt originally envisioned. In other words, the biggest single reason the Americans built the Canal in the first place was moot in less than 30 years. The Canal was now merely an auxiliary of the US Navy.

World War II also transformed the United States economy and solidified for all time the strength of both coasts. According to Bruce Cumings, the war remade the Pacific Coast of the United States. It created for the first time in human history a continental nation with a combined, integrated industrial economy from the Atlantic to the Pacific. And, "for the first time in American history, the Pacific States and much of the West were independent: in oil, steel, factories, and investment capital."[10]As the years went on, the Canal had less and less to do with all this. The

[6] Zadow p. 806–807.

[7] Noel Maurer & Carlos Yu *The Big Ditch: How America Took, Built, and Ultimately Gave Away the Panama Canal* (2011, Princeton University Press) p. 220–223.

[8] Captain R.S. Fahle, USN "The Panama Canal – An Auxiliary of the Fleet" *US Naval Institute Proceedings* (May 1954), p. 495.

[9] Ibid., p. 496.

[10] Bruce Cumings *A Dominion from Sea to Sea* (2009, Yale University Press) p. 333–334.

transformative changes in the domestic economy that had been unleashed during the war came to fruition in the postwar era. In the end, the evolution of the US Navy and the full industrialization of the Western United States, along with the greater integration of America's transcontinental railroads and the new Interstate Highway System, diminished the relevance of the Canal to both the US government and the American economy.

A Step Back: Making the American Century

To get a better sense of where the Canal has fit—and does fit today—we need to take a step back. It was World War II that finally launched the United States to pinnacles of power never seen before. Even prior to its entry into the war in 1941, America already possessed the world's largest economy, enjoyed the fruits of the dollar as the premiere currency of international trade, owned and operated the Panama Canal, contained the globe's financial and trade center, and produced and exported more oil than any other nation. America's further rise during the war would make it a superpower without challenge and one that remains so to the present.

By the end of World War II, the United States had emerged as more than just an economic superpower. Its military might was also unequaled. The US Navy reigned supreme on the seas and was the mightiest fleet ever to sail. America's aircraft patrolled the skies without any interference. The nation had already shown both the capacity to build an atomic weapon and, equally important, the will to use it. More than half of all the capital on planet Earth was in American hands. No country in history was ever so powerful. It is so today.

The simmering question for many leaders around the world was "What would America do with all of this power in its hands?" Much of the answer could be found in an essay written by Henry Luce just prior to America's entry into the war. It was entitled "The American Century." Luce was no ordinary American. He was probably one of the most influential private citizens of his day.[11] Luce's hold on American opinion cannot be overstated. A media magnate in the pre-television era, Luce's collection of publications was regularly read by tens of millions of Americans. *Time* summarized and interpreted the week's news. *Life* was a picture magazine of politics, culture, and society that dominated American visual perceptions and the nation's coffee tables. *Fortune* explored in depth the economy and the world of business. *Sports Illustrated* looked at the motivations and strategies of sports teams and key players. Counting his radio projects and newsreels, Luce built the first true multimedia empire.[12]

---

[11] Robert Edwin Herzstein *Henry R. Luce, Time, and the American Crusade in Asia* (Cambridge University Press, 2005) p. 1.

[12] Ibid.

In his February 1941 essay, which was published in *Life* 10 months *before* Pearl Harbor, Luce gave popular expression to America's place in the world. It laid the foundation for what eventually came to fruition.[13] Luce wrote that while America was not in the conflict—at least not yet—the nation was faced "with great decisions." He acknowledged America's almost endless wealth. "We know how lucky we are compared to all the rest of mankind. At least two-thirds of us are just plain rich compared to all the rest of the human family—rich in food, rich in clothes, rich in entertainment and amusement, rich in leisure, rich."

Luce was born in China to missionary parents. His zeal to make American values those of the world is evident. He observed that "America was fast becoming the sanctuary of the ideals of civilization. For the moment it may be enough to be the sanctuary of these ideals. But not for long." What Luce had in mind next would become much of the philosophy behind American Empire. "It now becomes our time to be the powerhouse from which the ideals spread throughout the world and do their mysterious work of lifting the life of mankind from the level of the beasts to what the Psalmist called a little lower than the angels."

Luce spoke for himself and other influential elites when he wrote, "It is only America as the dynamic center of ever-widening spheres of enterprise, America as the training center of the skillful servants of mankind, America as the Good Samaritan, really believing again that it is more blessed to give than to receive, and America as the powerhouse of the ideals of Freedom and Justice—out of these elements surely can be fashioned a vision of the Twentieth Century to which we can and will devote ourselves in joy and glad- ness and vigor and enthusiasm."[14] The missionary's call from Luce rippled across the country over the next years as America entered and fought World War II. Elite opinion would increasingly become shaped by Luce's notion of "The American Century."

The New Dealers Win the Day

It's good to remember that American zealots like Henry Luce were having a field day by the 1940s. Prior to World War II, the world had undergone the convulsion that was the Great Depression. Although references today abound whenever *we* enter a crisis—such as the inflation of the 1970s, the financial crisis of 2008, or the current COVID-19 pandemic—nothing in the modern era compares to the pain and suffering unleashed by the Great Depression. In the United States alone, unemployment regularly exceeded 30% for much of the 1930s. It was worse in Europe and downright terrible in other parts of the world. Unlike our time, there were few of any governmental programs to fall back on to relieve the pain.

[13] Henry Luce "The American Century" *Life*, February 17, 1941 http://www.informationclearinghouse.info/article6139.htm. Accessed January 22, 2022.

[14] Ibid.

The United States—with the arrival of Franklin Roosevelt into the White House in 1933—put in place a series of actions designed to help alleviate the suffering which was going on across the country. The New Deal was introduced and championed as the Federal government's package of pain relief. Programs like Social Security and the Citizen Conservation Corps ("The 3Cs") were meant to jumpstart the economy and help Americans get back on their feet. For the Roosevelt Administration, support from the American people of the original New Deal was so substantial that a Second New Deal was introduced in 1935. The New Deal appeared to be a great success. Unemployment continued to fall until to around 14% by 1937. Yet, the continued underlying weakness in the economy saw unemployment increase the next year to 19%. Still, the Roosevelt Administration claimed victory, and the New Deal was held up as a triumphant example of government intervention into the economy.

The belief that the Federal government could and should play an active role in the nation's economy created a generation of American leaders who adhered to this emerging philosophy. Prior to the New Deal, even the most progressive members of society saw the government's role in the economy as relatively limited. Now, as the test case of the New Deal unfolded, a growing movement made up of career civil servants, academics, and, increasingly, elected officials in the Democratic Party argued for the expansion of government power when it came to solving problems within the economy and beyond.

Henry Luce's zeal for "The American Century" was shared by many of these New Dealers, who occupied important positions across the US government and other important institutions. It was becoming a firmly held conviction that government power, if wielded in the right manner and direction, could ultimately become a force for good. This was the philosophy that formed the core of what many of America's leaders—including those in the Franklin Roosevelt Administration—sought when confronted with the incredible power that the nation had accumulated during World War II.

Bretton Woods and the American Century

It was kind to Luce's boyish joy that America *did* do something unique "in the course of human events" as the end of the war came into sight. Instead of going back to the antiquities-old playbook of the victors subjecting newly vulnerable peoples to vengeful punishments, the Americans shocked the world. The reveal of this took place in the summer of 1944 at a ski resort near Bretton Woods, New Hampshire.

Even as the war still raged on, the United States reached out to its weakened allies and invited them to send representatives to a conference to discuss America's plans for the postwar world. This was no mere act of hubris or arrogance. Everyone knew that this war, as all wars do, would eventually end. Except for a few holdouts in Germany and Japan, it was clear that the allies led by the Americans would ultimately triumph. And, it was evident that of all the allies, the United States would reign supreme. The other major allied nations were each significantly weakened by years of death and destruction. The Soviet Union, Britain, and France were frailer than they were before the shooting started. In the case of the Soviets, above 20 million of her citizens had already been killed. The British Empire was stretched beyond repair as the war dragged on. France suffered its third occupation by Germany in 70 years—and its navy was at the bottom of the Atlantic. Only the United States had seen its economic and military power expand.

For example, American oil production amounted in a total of six billion barrels, out of the total of seven billion barrels consumed by the allies during the conflict. This fueled an unmatched military buildup in world history. Between 1940 and 1945, the American Navy added 6700 new ships, of which 124 were aircraft carriers. The Merchant Marine added 34 million tons of new ocean cargo vessels. For the Army Air Corps and Navy, 324,000 aircraft were produced, including the War's most expensive single item: the B-29 Bomber. On the ground, the US Army and Marines Corps received 110,000 tanks and 2.4 million other military vehicles including military jeeps and trucks. All the while, the Manhattan Project harnessed atomic energy and developed nuclear weapons.[15]

President Roosevelt named Harold Ickes as Petroleum Coordinator for National Defense. During the war, Ickes worked closely with industry executives to oversee a 30% expansion in total oil production in the United States. This increase enabled the allies to secure the final push and achieve total victory over Germany and Japan.[16]

On one level, the Bretton Woods Conference was the culmination of a multiyear effort by the Americans and British to lay out the postwar international monetary system. Under the Atlantic Charter agreed to by Roosevelt and Churchill in 1941, the goal was embodied in the charter's fourth point that committed the United States and the Great Britain "to further the enjoyment by all States of access, on equal terms, to the trade and to the raw materials of the world which are needed for their economic prosperity." The fifth point further expressed a commitment to "the fullest collaboration between all nations in the economic field with the object of securing, for all, improved labor standards, economic advancement and social security" cooperation that would expand "production, employment, and the exchange and consumption of goods" and would reduce tariffs and other trade barriers.[17] Two new institutions—the International Monetary Fund and the International Bank for Reconstruction and Development (later the World Bank)—were to be built to help manage the achievement of these goals. For President Roosevelt and the US delegation which was made up of Secretary of State Cordell Hull; US Secretary of the Treasury Henry Morgenthau, Jr.; future Secretary of State Dean Acheson; and Henry Dexter White, a special assistant to the US Treasury, Bretton Woods was the New Deal played out on a global stage.

---

[15] These numbers were aggregated from Ian V Hogg *The American Arsenal: The World War II Official Standard Ordnance Catalogue* (Frontline Books, 2014).

[16] McNally *Crude Volatility: The History and the Future of Boom-Bust Oil Prices*, p. 92.

[17] US Department of State "The Bretton Woods Conference 1944" https://2001-2009.state.gov/r/pa/ho/time/wwii/98681.htm Accessed January 26, 2022.

The Conference began on July 1, 1944, and ran for 3 weeks, with 760 delegates from 44 allied nations in attendance. One might wonder: why Bretton Woods? Why a ski resort in the middle of the summer heat in the outer reaches of the New Hampshire mountains? Why not New York, where you could get a great dinner and see a Broadway show? Choosing a remote location for such an important meeting was deliberate. It allowed the hosts to control the narrative of the Conference and restrict access to only invited guests. Any snooping noses of the American press, the public, and the Congress could be quickly cut off.

The Conference was an exclusive affair. Some of the delegates in attendance would go on to become Presidents or Prime Ministers of the countries they represented, including Pierre Mendes of France, Louis St. Laurent of Canada, Walter Nash of New Zealand, and Pedro Espantoso of Peru. Others like Johan Willem Beyen of the Netherlands would later play a key role in building the European Union. Again, at this level, the Conference was intended to put the finishing touches on the Atlantic Charter and iron out the details around the postwar international monetary system.

Beneath the surface, however, there was a whole other set of considerations which required far greater attention. And, these considerations were much more relevant and visceral. The delegates wondered to themselves if much of the Conference was merely an academic exercise to justify the power grab that the Americans were sure to make at war's end. Using history as their guide, the delegates assumed the Americans would exploit their advantage and work to enrich themselves even more. This is what the Greeks, Romans, Carthaginians, and all other empires had precisely done after winning a great conflict. Why would the Americans be any different? Yet, the Americans *were* different.

The American Offer

Underneath the discussions around shiny new international institutions and monetary policies remained the real question of the conference: what are the Americans going to do with all their power? The answer to this question would determine everything that followed. In the end, the New Dealers representing the United States broke with the past and made clear to the attendees that they intended to do something *very* different.

The Americans laid out a four-part deal that was informally presented to the delegates over the course of 3 weeks. It constituted an offer from the Americans to all the allies. It was an offer, not a demand. The four parts of the deal included the following:

1. The Americans will use their massive military advantage to protect any nation who requests it.

This wasn't terribly surprising. Other conquering peoples had protected their allies in the past. What was different is that the Americans promised to pay for that protection. Moreover, this security guarantee was open-ended. There was no expiration date. The offer meant that any nation which came into the Bretton Woods system would not have to dedicate scarce resources to reconstituting their military capabilities: always an expense proposition. Instead, the Americans would provide for their defense and pay for it in perpetuity.

2. The Americans will open up their massive consumer market to any nation that accepted the deal.

To jumpstart their economies, the Americans encouraged the allies to focus on manufacturing. This way, large number of workers could be quickly put to work to make things. It could go a long way to alleviating the unemployment crisis so many were facing. But, the question begged: where would they sell all these manufactured goods? Consumers in most countries were facing years of poverty and food insecurity ahead. The US response was that foreign products and companies would have almost unrestricted access to the massive American market.

Since the end of the American Civil War, the US market had been far and away the biggest single prize for all sorts of businesses. The unparalleled combination of a secure continental island; almost unlimited natural resources, including oil; a dynamic system of capital creation and allocation; a culture of entrepreneurship; and, government policy that overwhelmingly encourages and supports capitalism made the United States unique in human history. These forces have blended in such a way that providence appears to be behind it all.

For each of the past 15 decades, despite recessions, depressions, crashes, and bubbles, the US economy was richer at the end of the decade than it was at the beginning. In fact, the rise of the United States as the dominant global economic force has been *the* business trend for the past 150 years. As John Steele Gordon observed, the United States became over a century ago—and remains today—"An Empire of Wealth." After Bretton Woods, any nation that wanted open access to the American market for their products and services just had to ask. They would be free to compete for American consumers against American companies and American workers on American soil.

3. In addition to the first two revolutionary elements, the Americans also provided massive financial stimulus to the Bretton Woods membership. Programs like the Marshall Plan jumpstarted much of Western Europe and Eastern Asia with trillions of free dollars with no strings attached. Later, the World Bank and International Monetary Fund would pick up the mantle and support economic development and growth around the globe.
4. To further sweeten the deal—if it wasn't already sweet enough—the Americans declared that under the banner of free trade, the movement of all goods on the world's oceans would be secured, and paid for, by the US Navy and the American

taxpayer. The concerns over supply chain security that had rattled so many for so long were now solved by the Americans seemingly forever.[18]

When the Americans laid out this deal, no one could believe their ears. Here was the most dominant nation in history saying that its strategic vision for the future was a world built on consumers and producers. And, incredibly, nearly all the costs and burdens of securing that vision would be borne not by the losers. Rather, the biggest winner of the war would do the heavy lifting for years to come. It all seemed good to be true. Yet, it was true.[19]

Without having to contend with Soviet aggression or worry about centuries-long rivalries with their neighbors, countries like the United Kingdom, France, West Germany, Japan, Taiwan, South Korea, and later India, Singapore, Thailand, China, and Vietnam could focus exclusively on rebuilding their economies. The security blanket provided by the United States ensured that business could be done without interference from others seeking to intrude on their growth.

A significant portion of their prosperity would come from exporting to the United States. The US market was made available to any nation who chose to participate. Later on the integration of China into the global economy initiated by President Nixon in 1972 and the collapse of the Soviet Union in 1990 assured for the foreseeable future that the dominant global idea would be capitalism as practiced in America.

Much of the world we live in today is, to a large part, the result of these conscious decisions undertaken by American political leaders at the end of World War II and beyond. The US basket of guarantees is one of the most effective and longest held promises in history. The results of America's gambit are clear. Since 1945, more people have lived safer, richer, and healthier lives than ever before. Wars between major powers are a distant memory. Extreme poverty—the scourge of the human experience—has been reduced by more than 90%.

In 1990, the United Nations created several targets under the name of Millennium Goals. Target 1.A was to "halve, between 1990 and 2015, the proportion of people whose income is less than $1.25 a day." In 1990, nearly half of the total human population lived in extreme poverty. Shocking everyone, this rate dropped to less than 10% by 2015. Today the total is around 6%. Even more incredible, this achievement happened during a period (1990–2015) when the global population increased by more than 2 billion human beings! Because of the American stabilization of the world since the end of World War II and the US' continued commitment to it, the United Nations has now realistically set a goal to eliminate *all* extreme poverty on the planet by 2030.[20] This achievement was not accomplished through increases in

[18] Andrew R. Thomas & Timothy J. Wilkinson *The Customer Trap: How to Avoid the Biggest Mistake in Business* (Apress; 2015) p. 56.

[19] Ibid. p. 67.

[20] Given the incredible progress made, the United Nations has set 2030 as the year when all extreme poverty can be eliminated. http://www.un.org/millenniumgoals/poverty.shtml, Accessed January 16, 2022.

foreign aid. Instead, it was the expansion of global economic growth underpinned by the American guarantees at Bretton Woods that made it happen.

Since the war, nations who in "normal times" would have needed to spend tremendous sums to rebuild their armies and navies instead were able to invest in improving the condition of their populations: i.e., schools, electricity, sanitation systems, and innovation. The American military assured peace. The American taxpayer paid the bill. The US Navy secured the world's shipping lanes. American taxpayers picked up that check, too. Products moved seamlessly around the world, unlike any time in the past. Open access to the US market assured a place to sell manufactured goods. Foreign companies and their workers benefitted immensely. National and business leaders built the "American cost savings" into their forecast models. Traditional expenditures on national defense and supply chain security—historically huge costs only digestible to the richest countries and firms—became negligible line items. America had the world's back.

Another Step Back: World War I and the Energy of American Ascendancy

The talk about "equal terms" and "collaboration" for "all Nations" with "the object of securing, for all, improved labor standards, economic advancement and social security" at Bretton Woods was nothing new. They had been banging around Europe and America for a while. One of the biggest adherents was US President Woodrow Wilson. Wilson's infamous "14 Points" after the end of World War I may have sounded eerily familiar to the delegates at Bretton Woods in 1944. The third point read: "The removal, so far as possible, of all economic barriers and the establishment of an equality of trade conditions among all the nations consenting to the peace and associating themselves for its maintenance." It would be America's assist in World War I and its rise as a superpower coming out of the war that made such rhetoric a future possibility.

Wilson's "14 Points": A Precursor to Bretton Woods

After the allied triumph over the Central Powers, America's position relative to other nations remained uncertain. As Ed Conway notes, America before the war was a "bit player" on the global stage relative to the other major powers.[21] Indeed, while America had passed Britain to become the world's largest economy sometime during the 1890s, US geopolitical influence and interest remained limited primarily to

[21] Ed Conway *The Summit Bretton Woods, 1944: J.M. Keynes and the Reshaping of the Global Economy* (Pegasus Books, 2014), p. 39.

the Western Hemisphere and the South Pacific. Although the first boat passed through the Canal in 1914, several years of tough work remained on the job. It wasn't until 1920, two years after the Great War ended, that the Canal became truly operational.

The Americans finally jumped into the European conflagration with a Declaration of War on April 2, 1917. Woodrow Wilson, who had been reelected a mere 5 months before on the slogan "At least he kept us out of war," orchestrated this leap into the European conflict. The 180-degree turn by Wilson and the events that followed sent shockwaves throughout the nation. At the time of its entry into the conflict, the US Army had only 200,000 active soldiers, of which 80,000 were National Guardsmen. The ranks would have to be expanded immediately. This was done through volunteer enlistments and conscription. The passage of the Selective Service Act in 1917 led to the registration of more than 24 million men to become eligible for the draft. Over the next 18 months (April 1917–November 1918), more than 4 million men served in the American Expeditionary Force, while another 600,000 served in the US Navy and 78,000 in the Marine Corps. In this relatively short period of time, 116,516 American service personnel were killed and 204,002 wounded.[22] As a point of reference, in the Vietnam War, which lasted from 1964 to 1973, more than 8.7 million Americans served in the armed forces. 58,220 military personnel were killed and 153,303 wounded.[23] Further, the total population of the United States in 1918 was 103.2 million; by 1973, it had more than doubled to 212 million. In short, World War I was a quick, yet bloody experience for the Americans.[24]

The scale and rapidity of death on the fields of France stunned many Americans. It quickly turned them sour on war in general and, later, their leadership and the European allies. President Wilson, on the other hand, sought to use the shocking brutality of the war to peddle an idealism grounded in international conflict resolution. Seeking to rebrand the conflict as "The War to End All Wars," Wilson poured all of his energies into establishing the League of Nations and getting his "14 Points" passed through Congress. After more than 6 months of negotiations in Europe, Wilson returned home in 1919 to see his future vision come crashing down. The American people—reeling from the bloodletting of their sons, brothers, and husbands—couldn't accept Wilson's overambitious global vision. Americans turned their backs on Europe's long history of self-destruction. Congress never ratified the "14 Points"; and, US interest in the political affairs of Europe evaporated away.

[22] Nese F. DeBruyne "American War and Military Operations: Lists and Casualties" *Congressional Research Service*, April 26, 2017, p. 2. https://fas.org/sgp/crs/natsec/RL32492.pdf. Accessed January 28, 2022.

[23] Ibid.

[24] U.S. Census Bureau, "History of the U.S. Population" https://census.gov/topics/population.html. Accessed January 28, 2018.

An Empire of Oil

Even after rejecting Wilson's plans for American leadership after the Great War, the nation did not withdraw back to its prewar isolationism. Quite on the contrary, America's coming of age as a superpower was now underway. The war saw to that. In 1914, the US dollar was quoted in fewer financial centers than the Italian Lira or Austrian Schilling.[25] London was the undisputed capital global financial hub, responsible for more than half of the entire world's exported capital, and financing most of the flow of international trade.[26] By 1919, Britain, in order to maintain its war effort, had liquidated 15% of all of its overseas investments, most of it to the United States. Also during the war, Britain and other allies also ran up tremendous debts to the US government, who had extended generous loans that eventually totaled $7 billion.[27] And, in addition to the overwhelming majority of oil that America provided the allies during the war, the United States also became the "factory and granary" to the world. American machinery and foodstuffs were shipped in ever-bigger quantities to the four corners of the world. By the mid-1920s, the torch had been passed. The dominant currency in the world was now the US dollar, having replaced British Sterling. The center of gravity of international trade, finance, and energy was now firmly in America.[28]

The manifestation of the United States as *the* main player on the global stage has paralleled the evolution of the Carbon Age. Prior to World War I, the primary sources for energy were wood, hydropower, steam, horses, and some coal. As the Great War commenced in 1914, oil remained mostly an afterthought in most planners' minds. There was an overabundance of it. Nevertheless, by 1919, when the Armistice was finally signed, things had changed inexorably. Recognized as a vital necessity for national survival, oil had become, in the elegant prose of the economist Julian Simon, "the master, or ultimate, resource."[29]

Experience during World War I educated leaders around the world that the future of their nations—and any other nation—would be incalculably shaped by its ability to secure oil. Increasingly mechanized armies and navies—airplanes, tanks, trucks, ambulances, other road vehicles, and, most importantly, ocean vessels—all operated on oil. A fleet of 827 motor cars and 15 motorcycles supported the British Expeditionary Force that went to France in 1914. By war's end in November 1918, the British army included more than 56,000 trucks, 23,000 motorcars, and 34,000 motorcycles, all powered by petroleum. Moreover, military aviation had burst on the scene to become the third dimension of warfare: after land and sea. Over the

[25] Barry Eichengreen *Exorbitant Privilege: The Rise and Fall of the Dollar and the Future of the International Monetary System* (Oxford University Press, 2011), p. 32.

[26] Conway, *The Summit Bretton Woods, 1944: J.M. Keynes and the Reshaping of the Global Economy*, p. 40.

[27] Ibid.

[28] Eichengreen, p. 32.

[29] Julian L. Simon *The Ultimate Resource* (Princeton University Press, 1981), p. 162.

course of the last 2 years of the war, Britain produced and deployed 55,000 planes; France, 68,0000 planes; Italy, 20,000; the United States, 15,000; and Germany, 48,000.[30]

By 1917, petroleum shortages were being experienced on all sides. Oil's availability now moved to the forefront of all military planning. The Interallied Petroleum Conference was established on the recommendation of the Interallied Conference at Paris in November. It consisted of representatives from the United States, the Great Britain, France, and Italy. Preliminary meetings were held in London as early as February 1918. The first formal meeting was delayed until May 6, 1918, when representatives from the United States could attend. The five sessions held during the war were in Paris, London, and Rome. Several subcommittees dealt with the following subjects: petroleum storage in France, standardization of petroleum products, an importation program in accordance with the schedule of the Allied Maritime Transport Council, and petroleum requirements of the allies in Europe and the Mediterranean.[31] The Committee's overall function was to agree upon the petroleum requirements of each ally, the best sources of supply, and specifications, tonnage, and routes for conveyance of oil supplies.[32]

By war's end, a new reality existed: oil had become a dominant force in shaping the operations and conduct of nations. This may have been best articulated by M. Henri Berenger, a French senator, industrialist, and writer, who served as his country's wartime Oil Commissioner and, later, was France's Ambassador to Washington: "He who owns the oil will own the world, for he will rule the sea by means of the heavy oils, the air by means of the ultra-refined oils, and the land by means of petrol and the illuminating oils. And, in addition to these, he will rule his fellow men in an economic sense, by reason of the fantastic wealth he will derive from oil—the wonderful substance which is more sought after and more precious today than gold itself."[33] Berenger's comments were more prescient that even he must have realized at the time. World War I was an inflection point. Prior to it, the movement of men and materials was accomplished by nineteenth-century means. During and immediately after the war, it became abundantly clear that oil had become the nurturing and sustaining resource for all nations.

The war marked the beginning of a large-scale *energy transition*, which, according to Vaclav Smil, is a "gradual shift from a specific pattern of energy provision to a new state of an energy system."[34] Such energy transitions are not to be taken lightly. The scope and magnitude of the fundamentals needed to develop the technical and infrastructural imperatives of an energy transition are enormous. There also

---

[30] Brian C. Black "How World War I Ushered in a Century of Oil", *The Conversation*, April 3, 2017, http://theconversation.com/how-world-war-i-ushered-in-the-century-of-oil-74585 accessed January 21, 2022.

[31] Ibid.

[32] John Weaver Frey, H. Chandler Ide, Eds. *A history of the Petroleum Administration for War, 1941- 1945* (U.S. G.P.O., 1946), p. 8.

[33] Timothy C. Winegard *The First World Oil War* (University of Toronto Press, 2016), p. 242.

[34] Vaclav Smil *Energy Transitions: History, Requirements, Prospects* (Praeger, 2010), p. vii.

exist abundant—and often unintended—social, political, and economic consequences during an energy transition that unfold, materialize, and, finally, need to be dealt with. Energy transitions are, therefore, protracted affairs, which take decades, not years, to be realized.[35]

Of course, oil had been used in a wide variety of ways for centuries prior to World War I. The Scriptures tell us of "oil out of flinty rock" (Deuteronomy 32:13) and "the rock poured me out rivers of oil" (Job 29:6). Dioscorides Pedanius, the Greek historian, detailed how the citizens of Agrigentum, in Sicily, burned oil in lamps prior to the birth of Christ. The ancient Egyptians used oil to prepare mummies, which were burned millennia later to operate locomotives across North Africa.[36] Nonetheless, new demands—first emanating from early twentieth-century military necessity and later from consumer-driven needs—accelerated the energy transition to oil and other carbon energy sources. It is this same energy transition that we are living through today.

The first oil well in America was drilled in 1859. Seventy years later, in 1919, following the Great War, one of the most popular business books in the country could state without hyperbole:

> *Petroleum is the fuel and lubricant of speed and mechanical efficiency- on land, on the sea, under the seas, in the air. Practically every human activity is dependent upon it to some degree. But it is only in the past decade that petroleum has really come into its own. This period has seen the perfection of the internal combustion engine, upon which the automobile, the aeroplane, the farm tractor, motorboats, the submarine, and many other efficient mechanical contrivances depend. Likewise, it has seen the beginning of an era of fuel oil for railway and marine transportation... Oil is now the new monarch of motion.*[37]

At the same time, fears—real or imagined—had convinced many that "peak oil" had been reached—that supply was soon to run out if new sources couldn't be found. Skyrocketing demand for oil during and immediately after the war left many wondering how long existing oil supplies could last. Global oil production before and during the war was overwhelmingly an American affair, with the United States accounting for more than 70% of all global output by 1918.[38]

Early on, the Americans recognized the significance of oil both during the war and its aftermath. Most of the other warring parties realized later that motor vehicles and fuel would become critical factors of military and, therefore, national importance. They neither established strategic oil reserves before August 1914, nor did they make serious efforts to raise the oil production in their own area of influence during the War. As the war ended, it was the Americans, followed later by everyone else, who led the scramble to find more oil.

While the United States was by far the biggest oil-producing nation in the world, domestic demand was rising much faster than supply. While exports to the allies

---

[35] bid., p. viii.

[36] John James McLaurin Sketches in *Crude Oil: Some Accidents and Incidents of the Petroleum Development in All Parts of the Globe* (Publisher: Author, 1896), p. 5.

[37] Reid Sayers McBeth *Oil: The New Monarch of Motion* (Markets Publishing Corp., 1919), p. 1.

[38] Ferdinand Friedensburg *Das Erdöl im Weltkrieg*, (Stuttgart, 1939) p. 121.

during the war consumed larger and larger quantities of US production, developments on the home front further placed huge expectations on domestic supply. The unprecedented mobilization that characterized America's entry into the war saw investment in new manufacturing and equipment more than quadruple: from $600 million in 1915 to $2.5 billion in 1918.[39]

By the end of the war, both business and consumers were eager to refocus. General Motors, for example, reported the number of cars, trucks, and tractors it sold for the first quarter in 1920 had risen 45.2% over the previous year.[40] General Motors' incredible growth was reflected in the broader automotive industry. Auto sales in America had quadrupled from 1909 to 1913 and then quadrupled again from 1913 to 1920. Americans bought 3.6 million cars in 1923, and by the end of the roaring 1920s, Americans owned 23 million private cars, out of a total population of 124 million people. In 1921, there were 387,000 miles of paved roads in the country. By 1929, there were 687,000 miles.[41] The "Monarch of Motion" was now evident for all to see.

American energy companies responded to the demand by lots of new drilling. Between 1915 and 1920, the number of wells drilled across the country increased to almost 34,000, and oil production soared by roughly 45%.[42] It is not hype to say that the Great War and the rise of an oil-centric economy transformed the United States. It would also be accurate to note that the war forced a penetrating reevaluation on how America would interact with the other nations of the world.

Like its economy, American foreign policy was stimulated by the war, yet in a different direction. The focus wasn't so much on "Mother Europe." Instead it was on places where oil could be located and extracted: oil that had quickly become the mother's milk of the American—and global—economies. The Monarch of Motion was now to significantly shape the course of US foreign policy.

The Unfolding Shape of American Empire

The American system of empire is much more a commercial one than others of the past. The establishment and growth of global capitalism is at its core. The resources of the US government and business are harnessed to that end. It benefits America and Americans to some extent. Yet, it benefits the greater world far more. In this

---

[39] Oliver Gilech: "Petroleum: 1914–1918-online". *International Encyclopedia of the First World War*, ed. by Ute Daniel, Peter Gatrell, Oliver Janz, Heather Jones, Jennifer Keene, Alan Kramer, and Bill Nasson, issued by Freie Universität Berlin, Berlin 2015-01-07. https://encyclopedia.1914-1918-online.net/article/petroleum accessed January 23, 2022.

[40] William Pelfrey *Billy, Alfred and, General Motors: The Story of Two Unique Men, a Legendary Company, and a Remarkable Time in American History* (AMACOM, 2006), p. 6.

[41] Ibid.

[42] Robert McNally *Crude Volatility: The History and the Future of Boom-Bust Oil Prices* (Columbia University Press, 2017), p. 53.

unique American aspect, actors as diverse as the Pentagon, CIA, the US Treasury, Federal Reserve, and Commerce Department, along with Wall Street bankers, manufacturers, transport firms, and retailers, tend to coalesce around sharing American economic practices abroad and, more generally, promoting free capital movement and open trade.

Governments everywhere play a key role in underpinning capitalism, such as maintaining property rights; overseeing contracts; resolving disputes, taxation, maintaining currencies; etc. It is the American government, however, that has played an exceptional role in the creation of a fully global capitalist system. It is the immense strength of US capitalism that made globalization possible. What continues to make the American government distinctive is its vital role in managing and superintending capitalism on a worldwide plane.[43]

The containment of Communism, whether in the Cold War in Europe or the very hot wars in East Asia in Korea and Vietnam, was largely about ensuring that as many of the world's states as possible would be open to the accumulation of capital. Moreover, America's assurances that oil flows from the Middle East and other energy-rich parts of the world were available to fuel international trade and the global economy additionally formed its Bretton Woods' guarantees. In summary, America overwhelmingly kept its word to the people of the world. Over decades, the elements of Bretton Woods became woven into the thinking-processes of corporate and national leaders everywhere. The outcomes were incredible. They still are. [44]

So, What About the Canal?

All this talk so far about World War I, the energy transition to the Carbon Age, the New Deal, World War II, Bretton Woods, the rise of the United States as *the* only superpower, etc. makes little mention about the Canal. This is not unintentional. The fact remains that the Canal—although remaining vital in many ways to global commerce we'll look at later—simply did not contribute much to any of this. In short, with or without the Canal of Panama, the United States would have become the most powerful nation in history.

For example, American political and business leaders embarked on a global quest together after World War I in search for overseas oil. It led them first to Mesopotamia, Mexico, Venezuela, the Dutch East Indies, Colombia, and Peru. As American diplomats were not highly specialized in regions outside of the Western Hemisphere, the pursuit for overseas oil didn't go well at first. The more experienced British and French in the Middle East and Sumatra outmaneuvered the Americans. In Mexico and South America, the United States did fare better,

[43] Sam Gindin and Leo Panitch, *The Making of Global Capitalism: The Political Economy of American Empire* (Verso Books, 2012), p. 16.

[44] Edward Conard *Unintended Consequences: Why Everything You've Been Told About the Economy Is Wrong* (Penguin, 2012) p. 14.

primarily due to its longstanding presence there, including in Panama. Meanwhile, vast new discoveries in California, Texas, and Oklahoma, coupled with the fresh supply from the Western Hemisphere, abated the threat of oil scarcity, and by 1924 a surplus had been created.[45] Overall, the contribution of the Canal to American energy security in the 1920s and beyond was negligible. Moreover, the full integration of the West Coast after World War II would have happened irrespective of the Canal.

This is *not* to say that the Canal failed to deliver any returns on the significant investment the Americans initially made to build it. It was just that those returns didn't justify holding on to the Canal forever.

The Apollo Moon Program and the Panama Canal: Offspring From the Same Father

The many years I have spent thinking about the future of the Canal of Panama found me discovering similarities between America's approach to the Apollo Moon Program. In 2012, I coauthored a book about the ignominious end of Apollo. The focus of that book was on the Saturn V rocket: specifically the one that is prominently displayed today at Kennedy Space Center. If you haven't visited it, be sure to make a trip to do so the next time you are in Central Florida. It will be well worth your time and effort.

Many of the components and stages from that rocket were originally planned for the Apollo 18 mission. Unfortunately, that mission—and the four others scheduled to follow Apollo 18—were all cancelled almost immediately after Neil Armstrong put his footprints on the Moon in July 1969. America had now been there, done that, and got the T-shirt. Captain Gene Cernan, the Last Man on the Moon and the Commander of Apollo 17, graciously wrote the book's Foreword.[46] Since Gene left the Moon's surface in 1972, no human beings have returned to the deep reaches of space beyond near-Earth orbit.

Between Armstrong's Apollo 11 mission and Cernan's Apollo 17, public interest and political support for the Apollo Program cratered. If you've seen Tom Hanks in the movie "Apollo 13," there is an accurate portrayal of his character Astronaut Jim Lovell valiantly trying to convince a group of congressional leaders on why it was important to continue support for the Moon Missions. It is believed that Armstrong's walk on the Moon was the most watched event in human history. By April 1970, a mere 9 months after the first moonwalk, American TV networks barely covered the lead up to the Apollo 13 mission. When something went wrong 2 days after liftoff

[45] Gerald D. Nash *United States Oil Policy, 1890-1964: Business and Government in Twentieth Century America* (University of Pittsburgh Press Digital, 1968), p. 49.

[46] Andrew R. Thomas, Paul N. Thomarios, Foreword by Gene Cernan *The Final Journey of the Saturn V* (2012; University of Akron Press).

and it looked like the astronauts might not make it back home, the world was once again riveted to their TV screens. The human drama of three brave men facing imminent death was too much to ignore. Nevertheless, after the tremendous effort that successfully bought Lovell and his crew safely home, Americans once again seamlessly turned their attention away from the Apollo Program.

The Apollo 18 rocket and the other remaining $1 billion Saturn V rockets that had already been built and paid for were eventually broken up, disassembled, or worse. These giants of the sky—363 feet in height, which horizontally in America's most common measurement scale includes endzone, football field, and the other endzone—exceeded many records in human flight and aviation: the greatest amount of thrust ever generated, the most powerful engines ever used, a perfect launch record, and many more. Yet, instead of going on a 250,000-mile trip to the Moon, the final journey of Apollo 18 covered only 1.9 miles and took more than 20 years.

Around 1975, the massive Saturn V was simply laid out in the parking lot in front of the Vehicle Assembly Building—at that time the largest structure in the world. The rocket endured Florida's harsh sun, humidity, and hurricanes—but just barely for more than 20 years. Occasionally, a coat of paint would be slapped on to keep it presentable to the visitors on the bus tour and cover up the mold and mildew. Still, it was rotting from the inside and out.

Fortunately in 1995, under the leadership of the Smithsonian Institution, a plan was put in place to restore and preserve the rocket to its original condition and house it in the new Apollo/Saturn V Center. Selected to do the work was my great friend Paul Thomarios—the son of Greek immigrants from Akron, Ohio. In May 1996, Thomarios completed the project, and the refurbished Saturn made the journey from the parking lot to its permanent home, where it continues to dazzle more than 1.5 million visitors at Kennedy Space Center each year.

Like the building of the Saturn V rocket, which took mankind on its greatest adventure, the completion of the Canal of Panama is easily recognized as one of its greatest engineering feats. Nevertheless, I can't help but see the parallels in the way America treated both undertakings over time.

It is not a leap to say that without the force of the US Presidency behind each of these ambitions, neither one would have ever gotten started. As the famous Roman dictum reminds us: *Intitum didium facti.* The start *is* half the deed. Both Teddy Roosevelt and John Kennedy used the power of the bully pulpit along with the sheer force of their personalities to convince the Congress to fund these massive projects. The fact that majorities in both Chambers went on nearly blind faith and dedicated huge sums of national treasure to projects that had never been done before is a testament to salesmanship of the highest order.

Neither of these visions lacked important reference points. It wasn't a case of merely shooting in the dark. The success of the Panama Railroad provided some key insight for Roosevelt as to the scale and magnitude of the work required there. For Kennedy, America's already well-developed nuclear ballistic missile program was a basic roadmap to Apollo.

Nevertheless, there remained many "known unknowns" and "unknown unknowns" to make both happen. Hundreds, if not thousands, of questions needed answers. Many of them led to more questions. At Panama, for example, would the Canal be a sea-level or lock chamber design? How would the dirt from the Culebra Cut be removed? What was the plan for dealing with the yellow fever and malaria that racked the Isthmus? etc. To get a man to walk on the Moon and bring him safely back to the Earth by the end of the 1960s was equally daunting. New materials, manufacturing processes, engineering designs, and communication capabilities that had not yet been created would be needed to get it done. And, of course, the big question for each project: how much would each of these finally cost? No one really knew. How could they? Still, the Presidents, majorities in the Congress, *and* the American people jumped in anyway. Roosevelt and Kennedy both garnered large-scale support for their ambitions by connecting the Canal and the Moonshot to national security and American Ascendancy.

Using Manifest Destiny as the foundation for his argument, Roosevelt claimed that the Canal was needed to make America a truly global player: to achieve the fulfillment of its natural evolution whose time had come. Doing so would allow the US Navy to project power more easily. Further, the Canal would fully open up Asia's markets to America.

For Apollo, in the context of the Cold War and the Nuclear Age, Kennedy asserted that space would be the next frontier. If the Soviets could gain an upper hand in the outer reaches, what would that mean for America's ability to defend itself and the allies here on Earth? It other words, it was America's right and Manifest Destiny to dominate space, too.

It is a fascinating paradox that what Roosevelt and Kennedy didn't know—and couldn't have known—was that their dreams be would quickly superseded by their primary motive: American Ascendancy. In other words, by the time the Canal was finished and man had walked on the Moon, America's unstoppable rise had made both accomplishments almost pyrrhic victories. This is never to say that constructing the Panama Canal and sending 12 men to live in another world and safely returning them home were not beyond awesome. They are. I wouldn't have spent so many precious years of life thinking, writing, and researching on these topics if I didn't get goosebumps, a tear in my eye, and the pride that comes from being an American every time I see at a massive ship navigating the Canal or when I stand under the Saturn V rocket at Kennedy Space Center. Each of these alone represents some of the best things about my country and—maybe a stretch here—our collective humanity.

History, however, is not so sentimental. In both cases, by the time the original objectives had been accomplished (building the Canal and walking on the Moon), America was already moving on. The country checked the box and, then, mostly forgot. It took longer for the Canal than Apollo to lose its luster, yet the final destination for both was pretty much the same.

Chapter 3
A Success Story: Made in Panama

I have no idols. I admire work, dedication and competence.

—Ayrton Senna

The greatest leader is not necessarily the one who does the greatest things. He is the one that gets other people to do the greatest things.

—Ronald Reagan

Try not to become a man of success. Rather become a man of value.

—Albert Einstein

A good engineer is a person who makes a design that works with as few ideas as possible. There are no prima donnas in engineering.

—Freeman Dyson

At this moment, several ships are transiting through the Canal of Panama. Hundreds of people are making sure that these ships transit from one ocean to another in a safe, efficient, and reliable way. Traffic control personnel, pilots, tugboat captains, engine officers, locomotive operators, sailors, boat operators, cable passers, administrative personnel, security teams, and many others work 24/7/365 to make such a complex maneuver so seem simple. With all due respect to Beethoven, Mozart, and Bach, the orchestration of the Canal is far more complicated and precise than anything the great composers could have imagined.

Bluntly stated, Panama's ability to manage the Canal has become one of the best examples of ongoing management excellence anywhere. By every reasonable measure, the Panamanians have outshined the Americans who constructed, operated, and, ultimately, handed over the Canal. Whether through the lens of record profits, higher customer satisfaction, viable innovation, improved efficiencies, workforce satisfaction, better safety, increased transits, or sustainability, Panama's and the Canal's results over the past 20-plus years speak for themselves.

A. R. Thomas, *The Canal of Panama and Globalization*,
https://doi.org/10.1007/978-3-031-05152-4_3

Optimism About Panama Wasn't Always So High

Interestingly, as Panama—and the rest of the world—looked to the formal handover of the Canal and all its related infrastructure on January 1, 2000, serious doubts remained as to how this small nation would approach this awesome responsibility. Many skeptics emerged, including in Panama, believing that the country had neither the necessary resources nor the ability for such a massive undertaking. As the handover approached, critics likened the Americans giving the Canal to Panama to a father giving the keys of the Ferrari to his teenage son while saying something like "don't screw it up." And, while many of the skeptics were irrational in their outright dismissal of Panama's prospects for effectively managing the Canal, there were some legitimate concerns.

At the top of the list was the future of the Panamanian government. Just a few years earlier, in December 1989, the United States "invaded" Panama to get rid of Manuel Noriega: a sadistic dictator who, in a matter of 5 years, had turned the country into a quasi-narco state.[1] The nullification of the legitimate victory of Guillermo Endara in the May 1989 elections—and the continuous demonstrations against the Noriega regime that followed—triggered the dictator into wider even crackdowns against any dissent. And, while Noriega had become the "pineapple face" of the political turmoil, violence, and repression, which were now hallmarks of Panamanian life, all of this had started much earlier.[2]

In 1968, Lt. Colonel Omar Torrijos seized power 11 days after the popular election of Arnulfo Arias to the presidency. For much of the next two decades, Panama would see a series of popularly elected presidents come and go, while real power increasingly moved to the hands of military leaders like Torrijos and Noriega.[3] Still, it was Torrijos—who by 1977 had removed all pretense of democracy and simply declared himself Head of State—that negotiated the treaties with US President Jimmy Carter. Even the staunchest supporters of Carter were concerned that it was an unelected military autocrat with whom the Americans were dealing.

[1] "Operation Just Cause" was the removal of Manuel Noriega and the destruction of the FDP, the Spanish acronym for the Panamanian Defense Forces, which constituted Noriega's thugs and henchmen. While labeled an invasion in the press and the George H.W. Bush Administration, "Operation Just Cause" was conducted primarily from the Canal Zone next to Panama City. Elements of Special Forces and the 82nd Airborne Division were transported to Panama from the United States. Still, much of the logistical support and command and control came from within the cozy confines of the Zone. One of the best books on the subject is Enrique Chuez, *Operation Causa* (Centro de Estudios Latinoamericanos; Panama, 1991).

[2] Noriega was called "Cara de Pina" behind his back: "Pineapple face" in English, for his pot-marked face. A must-read biography on Noriega is J. Scott Bronstein's *Noriega's Ghost* (Debate; New York, 2018).

[3] After Independence from Colombia in 1903, early Panamanian democracy was a struggle. Despite a new Constitution, there were few institutions the new nation possessed that could serve as foundations for popular consent. These critical building blocks had to be constructed from scratch. It was not going to be easy. A good place to start for an overview of Panamanian political development is Robert C. Harding's *The History of Panama* (Greenwood; Westport, CT. 2006).

This unfortunate history was easily recalled when, immediately after the removal of Noriega, the United States installed Guillermo Endara in the presidency: where he served his 5-year term. Prohibited to run for a second term by Panama's constitution, it was expected that Endara would turnover power to the newly elected president in 1994. That election, Panama's first since the removal of Noriega, was won by Ernesto Balladares, with a plurality of a mere 33.3% of the popular vote. A founding member of the political party PRD with a long history to Torrijos, Balladares had been appointed by the General as Treasury Minister in 1976. PRD, the Spanish acronym for Revolutionary Democratic Party, was founded by Torrijos and others in 1970 to legitimize his power.

Balladares oversaw the 1989 election that Endara had won, but Noriega dismissed. After the US invasion, thousands of PRD leaders and supporters—not Balladares though—were arrested or punished; and, it was believed the party was likely finished. Nevertheless, Balladares' narrow victory revealed the PRD still had a lot of life in it.[4] Understandably, outsiders and insiders both were more than a little vexed to see the party of Torrijos and Noriega return to power, albeit legitimately, so close to the agreed handover of the Canal.

By the early 1990s, it was quite reasonable to wonder whether critical democratic institutions, which were being reestablished in Panama, would be up to the challenge of receiving the Canal and all of its infrastructure by the end of the decade. This was a big unknown. Beyond the viability of the Panamanian state, a second major worry around the future of the Canal was its defining role in Panamanian society. Legitimate questions such as "Would the Canal be a reflection of the best of ALL of Panamanian society?", "How would the benefits from the Canal be shared with ALL Panamanians?", and, worryingly, "Might the Canal ultimately just become another asset of the country's long-standing elite?" were being raised.

The Panamanians moved right away to assuage the doubters. In 1992, Endara appointed Joaquín José Vallarino, who was a member of the Board of Directors of the Panama Canal Commission, to direct the process of designing a constitutional amendment around the future of the Canal and its relationship with the Panamanian people. Preparing a new amendment was a complex process in those early days of born-again democracy. It had to be approved, according to one of the mechanisms established by the existing Panamanian Constitution, in two successive terms of the legislature. That is, it had to be passed during the administrations of Endara and whoever came next. In this case, it was Balladares.

The amendment needed to be done as quickly as possible so as to avoid the politization of the Canal and to get needed revenues from the Canal into the national treasury.

On December 27, 1993, the first legislative assembly approved the new amendment. It would then have to be approved by the next legislature without any change. It was. This last legislative act gave life to the Panama Canal Authority (ACP). The

[4] The best book in English on Panamanian politics over the past 50 years is Michael J. Conniff and Gene E. Bigler's *Modern Panama: From Occupation to Crossroads of America* (Cambridge University Press; Cambridge, UK, 2019).

amendment achieved its mission of setting the essential standards for the management of the water route under the principles of independence from partisan politics. It also provided the new Authority with managerial objectives aimed at promoting labor excellence and, therefore, strengthening the merit system of advancement. The Amendment was also on target precisely by adjusting to global maritime trends. The Amendment to the Constitution anticipated the behavior of the industry its serves as well:

> *An autonomous legal person of Public Law is created, which will be called the Panama Canal Authority, to which the administration, operation, conservation, maintenance and modernization of the Panama Canal and its related activities will correspond exclusively, in accordance with the constitutional norms and laws in force, so that it works in a* ***safe, continuous, efficient and profitable*** *manner. It will have its own patrimony and the right to administer it.*

The proof of the success of "Title XIV of the National Constitution" can be seen in that ACP has resisted for more than two decades the forces of outside political interference.[5]

What You Want in a Leader

The quiet competence and dedication to their job that so many Panamanian workers have demonstrated prior to and since the handover of the Canal might be best embodied in Jorge Luis Quijano. For 44 years, Quijano worked for the Canal in a wide range of positions, finally finishing his career as CEO of the ACP from 2012 to 2019. Prior to becoming CEO, he was designated to manage the Panama Canal's $5.25 billion Expansion Program; and, to that effect, he was appointed Executive Vice President of the Engineering and Programs Management Department.[6]

Under the Expansion Program, he headed a group of professionals in charge of contracting and managing the critical components of the Locks Design and Construction contract; the Atlantic and Pacific entrance channels dredging contracts, the contracting of four dry excavation contracts to create a new 6.1 km inland channel that would connect the lake level navigation channel to the upper level of the new locks in the Pacific end of the Canal; the lake level dredging to be performed mainly by the ACP workforce; and numerous other smaller support contracts.

As humble as he is smart, Quijano was born in Panama City in 1952. He came from a generation of Panamanians whose parents wanted them to pursue either medicine, the law, or engineering. Quijano's father—who had studied architecture—was stationed as Consul General in various countries around the world, including Port Said, Egypt. For young Jorge, seeing the Suez Canal up close and

[5] Juan Pablo Fábrega "Regimen Juridico de La Autoridad del Canal de Panama" White Paper, November 2016.

[6] Sr. Jorge Luis Quijano was gracious to provide the time for several interviews with the author over the course of 2021.

getting to travel on a ship with his Dad as it entered the Suez Canal from the Mediterranean Sea remains an unforgettable experience. In January 1964, Jorge joined his parents and younger brothers in Yokohama, Japan, where his father had received a new assignment. Just 2 weeks prior to Jorge's departure to Japan, on January 9, 1964, Panama experienced the most significant anti-US protests up to that time. Pictures were splashed on front pages around the world of American police and soldiers shooting young demonstrators as they tried to fly the Panamanian flag over the Canal Zone. In a first, Panama broke off diplomatic relations in protest over the killings of the students.

Interestingly, Quijano was able to register and attend a US Air Force School in Yokohama. Not long after, the family moved once again, this time to Malaysia, staying until the coup led by Omar Torrijos that overthrew the election of Arnulfo Arias forced the family to return. Upon returning to Panama, Quijano enrolled at the Panama Canal College, a school operated by the Americans inside the Canal Zone. During his first 2 years as an undergraduate, he thrived especially in physics, mathematics, and the emerging field of computer science. As he prepared to transfer to complete his degree, it was clear that Quijano would study engineering, likely somewhere in Texas. The big questions were: why and exactly where?

The answer to the "why" was because of a girl. Quijano's girlfriend at the time, Marcia, had transferred to continue her physical therapy studies at Texas Women's University in Denton, just outside of Dallas. Quijano wanted to be close to Marcia. So, he initially applied and was accepted at Texas Tech, University of Texas in El Paso, and University of Texas in Arlington. In the end, however, Texas Tech in Lubbock was too cold, while UT El Paso was too far from Denton. Moreover, Quijano's father nixed UT Arlington because it was too *close* to Denton and any possible distractions from Marcia. The combination of cold, distance, and Dad's wishes forced another option: Lamar University in Beaumont, which is closer to Houston. It worked out well on every front. Quijano remains one of Lamar's most famous alumni. He earned both a BS and Master of Engineering in Industrial Engineering there and has been married to Marcia for more than 47 years.

After receiving his Master's, Quijano returned home to Panama and found a job as an engineer at Refinería Panamá SA, a division of the Texaco oil company, in Bahía Las Minas in the province of Colón. Daily, he carpooled an hour and a half each way with some colleagues across the Isthmus from his home in Panama City: an arduous commute to say the least on a twisting two-lane road. Quijano worked as a process engineer at the refinery for a year and a half, a time when the Canal was in American hands and the Canal organization was going through lots of upheaval.

The possibility of working for the Panama Canal Company had never really crossed Quijano's mind until a friend who worked in human resources for the US Armed Forces in Panama encouraged him to apply for a job there. An early riser due to his long, daily commute, Quijano showed up 10 min in advance for his 7:00 am interview at the Pedro Miguel Locks: surely surprising his prospective employers. A month later, Quijano was offered a job not in the Army but at the Panama Canal. He has never looked back.

Starting in Trying Times

In December 1975, he entered as an industrial engineer in charge of scheduling the maintenance of the three Canal locks. At that time, the negotiations around what would later be called Torrijos-Carter Treaties were nearing a critical stage—and there was a lot of tension between the Panamanians and Americans who worked on the Canal. The Treaties were focused on creating the basis for a smooth and seamless handover of the Canal and all the surrounding infrastructure to Panama, along with the progressive withdrawal of all military bases from Panama. The normal onboarding process for any new hires was a rigorous 8-week introduction to the Canal. Yet, that was not case for Quijano. His new American bosses did not give him the usual time to learn and adjust to the new job. They merely placed Quijano in an office and told him on Day 1: "You just go out to do the tasks or projects we assign you. You can't be out there in orientation because we've just gone through a major downsizing and you're the only one we're hiring."

He quickly figured out that much of his new job was "to achieve greater efficiencies," which could be translated into possibly more layoffs. Immediately, he felt the rejection of workers whose jobs were on the chopping block. The view that "here comes this new, young Panamanian to cut off our heads" was abundantly clear from his American colleagues. Add this to the anxiety over the Treaty negotiations and it was a potentially volatile mix. This is how his career in the Canal began.

In the next few months, the level of internal animosity within Canal operations reached a boiling point. During the scheduled maintenance of the culvert valves that control the water flow to raise and lower vessels at the Miraflores Locks in 1976, the American-led team of craftsmen began the work but then slowed down the process of reinstallation of the valve machinery: causing massive delays to the transit of the vessels through the Canal. This was a not-so-subtle message from the American workers at the Canal to the US team negotiating the Treaties: don't give away our Canal! For Quijano and his Panamanian colleagues, it was extremely stressful to enter the culverts deep in the lock walls and encounter a group of American workers who were certain that he was there to achieve additional reductions in staffing. Thankfully nothing but some mumbled words and long, hard stares came from it.

The two Treaties to handover the Canal to Panama were finally signed on September 7, 1977, in a ceremony with Jimmy Carter, Omar Torrijos, and many other dignitaries. The one treaty is officially titled "The Treaty Concerning the Permanent Neutrality and Operation of the Panama Canal" and is commonly known as the "Neutrality Treaty." Under this agreement, the United States retained the permanent right to defend the Canal from any threat that might interfere with its continued neutral service to ships of all nations. The other is titled "The Panama Canal Treaty" and stated that on December 31, 1999, Panama would assume full control of Canal operations and become primarily responsible for its defense. This was underpinned by the provision that the transition and handover to Panamanian control would officially begin on October 1, 1979.

Celebrations broke out across Panama, yet the deal was yet not done. To make everything official, the people of Panama had to approve both Treaties, which they did 6 weeks after the signing ceremony with a two-thirds majority of the popular vote on each one. Next, it was left to the US Senate to fulfill its constitutional responsibility of Advise and Consent, which it did, voting 68-32 on March 16, 1978, to approve both treaties. Nevertheless, there remained strong, vocal opposition in the United States to the Treaties, particularly in the House of Representatives. While the Treaties were now official as a result of the Senate's vote, the loud criticism of the Treaties by their opponents across the United States cast a broad shadow over the long-term viability of the handover. Many in Panama were concerned that since it was going to take more than 20 years to implement the main Treaty, a future American Administration could ultimately negate the agreements. This caused great uncertainty on the ground, as neither the Panamanians nor the Americans who worked for the Canal knew what was really going to happen.

Still, in the short term at least, the Panama Canal Company was changed to the Panama Canal Commission—a Federal Agency of the United States under the Secretary of Defense and attached to the Secretary of the Army. It had the task of initiating the transition and completing the transfer of the Canal within a period of 20 years and 3 months, until December 31, 1999. The task was to be carried out jointly between the two countries to reduce the anxiety of the Canal's clients.

While many frontline American workers and even some in the administration on the Canal held out hope that the Treaties would somehow be nullified, there were even larger numbers of Americans who set out from Day 1 to make the handover a success for both countries. Quijano had the fortune of working with American supervisors and managers who were very committed to the process. They said, "Here is a mandate, we must implement those Treaties and we must give space to the Panamanians"; and it was there that they began. As a result, new opportunities opened up for Panamanians in larger supervisory and managerial roles, and, in Quijano's case, that meant he could now rise in the Locks Division, which was one of the most complex areas of Canal operations and where there had been significant American control since all managerial positions there were considered security positions, which only US citizens could hold.

The 1980s were hectic years on the Canal. With the 1999 deadline looming, there was lots of work to do. First and foremost, it was critical to ramp up the number of Panamanians working across all areas of Canal operations. For example, in 1979, there were only 2 Panamanian pilots out of a total of almost 300. The pilots perform a vital function: upon entering the Canal, it is a pilot who maneuvers and navigates a vessel while transiting the waterway. The training to be a pilot is intense. Years of study and hands-on training are needed to learn the basics of the job. Then, another 8 years are required to achieve a level of expertise and certification that allow a pilot to transit the largest ships on the Canal by themselves.

Since his arrival at the Canal, Quijano had been scheduling maintenance in the Canal's three locks (Gatun, Pedro Miguel, and Miraflores) yet intermittently relieved the American managers when they went on leave. In 1984—after almost 10 years on the job—he was promoted to Maintenance Manager of the Pacific Locks (Pedro

Miguel and Miraflores). Two years later, Quijano was promoted again to lead a group of locks engineers to evaluate technical and maintenance issues on all the locks. This position was also focused on programmatic elements such as budgets, capital investments, and leading research and development and new projects. Quijano stayed in that job from 1986 to 1989. He was then selected as manager of the entire Locks Division, in charge of more than 1300 workers across the entire Canal.

It was on December 20, 1989, when the US military intervention in Panama occurred. The operation ended on January 3, 1990, with the delivery of Manuel Antonio Noriega to the US troops. While military operations ended relatively quickly, the country was paralyzed for 40 days. The Canal, on the other hand, only stopped its operations for a few hours in the early morning of the first day. Both the American and Panamanian workers did their jobs and assured the global community that nothing would stop the safe and reliable passage of ships: a tradition that has been kept until today.

Facing the Resistance

The 1990s were supposed to lay the foundations for the delivery of the Canal to Panama "in the best possible condition" as was promised in the Torrijos-Carter Treaties. The existing infrastructure to be transferred was massive: nearly 580 square miles of land that included some 7000 buildings, such as military facilities, warehouses, schools, and private residences and, of course, the Canal itself. The highly aggressive natural environment of Panama requires significant and regular capital investment in maintenance. The brutal heat, humidity, blistering tropical sun, deep jungles, and annual rainfalls averaging over 8–14 feet per year breathe regular life into rust, mold, and corrosion. Unfortunately, despite this reality, some US leaders within the Canal organization were unwilling to support large outlays on maintenance because the American departure was now less than 10 years away. Their belief was to wait until Panama took over and then let the Panamanians deal with it.

To force the Americans to carry out the promised investments required to properly operate and maintain the Canal, Quijano and others formed a small group of key Panamanians that was later called "La Matraca" (which means "rattle" in Spanish). The purpose of the group was to make some noise. According to Quijano, the group had already gained some ground by using their participation in the Ad-Hoc Commission for the Constitutional Amendment for the Panama Canal to outline their concerns about the overall state of the infrastructure. They clearly felt that changes in the investment pattern toward maintenance, replacement of obsolete equipment, and improvements of the infrastructure were moving in the wrong direction; and, this clearly did not bode well for the future.

To build a bridge to the Panamanian members of the Board of Directors of the PCC, "La Matraca" engaged a dozen Panamanians who were working in a variety of functions within the Canal to join the effort to neutralize the resistance of the

American holdouts. In 1995, Quijano and Rodolfo Sabonge, another founding member of La Matraca, were able to meet with the then Chancellor of the Republic, Gabriel Lewis Galindo, at his home. He was given a draft letter that was addressed to the president of the Board of Directors of the PCC. The letter proposed an infrastructure audit in order identify the necessary investments and improvements to ensure that Panama would receive the Canal in good condition. The audit would be conducted by an independent Swedish government agency that did this kind of consulting work.

Eventually, the Panamanian directors of the PCC presented the proposal to the entire Board. The American Joe R. Reeder, who had assumed the position of President of the binational Board of Directors, agreed with the idea of a proposed audit. Still, Reeder mandated that the US Corps of Engineers would carry it out.[7] In response to Reeder's move, the Panamanian members of the Board created a parallel entity—the Blue Ribbon Engineering Committee—to conduct the audit. The committee was made up of prestigious Panamanian engineers such as Alberto Alemán Zubieta—who accepted the challenge of leading it—along with Roberto Roy, Moisés Castillo De León, Ernesto Jordán, Álvaro Palacios, and Carlos Moreno. There remained attempts to obstruct the audits of both the US Army Corps of Engineers and the "Blue Ribbon Engineering Committee" by some American holdouts. Nevertheless, despite the resistance, the Panamanians got the US government to promise to fund more than $1 billion in Canal improvements and maintenance beginning in 1996.

Still, to make sure the Americans kept their word—akin to a "Trust, but verify" approach—some members of "La Matraca," including Quijano, presented the recommendations of the USACE-Blue Ribbon Committee at the Universal Congress of the Interoceanic Canal. In addition to detailing some of the projects that were already underway, the team shared the results of independent studies that indicated the Canal must consider an expansion of the locks. A failure to expand the lock system would likely consume the remaining capacity of the Canal and remove any opportunity to adapt to a rapidly changing global economy. In the end, as the transfer deadline approached, the Americans kept their word. It was becoming clear that Panama was going to receive a well operating Canal undergoing a multifaceted major improvement program on the most important infrastructure elements. The question was quickly becoming: how well would the Panamanians do once they fully took over?

[7] It should be noted that during his term as Chairman of the Board of Directors of the PCC, Joe Reeder was a great ally of the Panamanians. The early retirement of several resisting, senior-level Americans during his tenure was "encouraged" by Reeder. This greatly enhanced the transition process by allowing Panamanians to fill these roles years prior to the transfer. Further, Reeder instituted a clear mandate to the entire Board of Directors of "one team—one mission," which permeated throughout the culture of the PCC.

The Canal Transfer: An Unequivocal Triumph

In mid-1999, Quijano became Vice President of Maritime Operations: this meant he was now responsible for all the traffic activity of the intercontinental aquatic highway, including the locks operations and maintenance. A few months later, the Panamanian flag was finally raised alone on the flagpole in front of the steps of the Canal Administration Building, which remains the offices of the ACP until today. Quijano remained in his role until 2007. During this period, the global shipping industry unanimously agreed that Panama's level of service and maintenance standards of the Canal exceeded those of their American predecessors. At the same time, the industry absorbed Panama's new pricing formula, which focused on increasing revenues by charging for the real value of the route. As a result, in the years after the Panama takeover, the Canal broke records in tonnages, income, and profitability.

Critical to this initial success was the establishment of global standards of operating the Canal. A big part of Quijano's job was to meet the requirements for earning the ISO-9001 designation: the international standard that specifies requirements for a quality management system (QMS). Organizations use the ISO-9001 standard to demonstrate their ability to consistently provide products and services that meet customer and regulatory requirements. Interestingly, under the United States, the Canal had never achieved the ISO-9001 standard. The Panamanians clearly understood achieving it would prove to the world that the Canal was operating at full efficiency with the highest levels of quality assuredness. Further, ISO-9001 validation would allow for the Panamanians to expand the Canal's offerings to a larger market with regular price increases, which would lead to greater tonnage each year and, ultimately, increased revenues. Quijano got to work right away on the herculean effort of assembling and managing a multidisciplinary team from across the operations and human resources departments to create the needed internal infrastructure to achieve the standard. Within a very short period, less than 2 years, the Canal was awarded ISO-9001 status on May 15, 2001.

Reaching the ISO-9001 threshold immediately opened up enhanced communication with the Canal's stakeholders and clients around the world. A "dialogue of equals" now existed with shipping companies, cargo importers and exporters, producers, and the ports that the ships use. No one anywhere could look at the seriousness and dedication of the Panamanians to make the Canal better and not be impressed. The results speak for themselves: between 2000 and 2005, when the Canal was under Panamanian control, it was able to pass on $1.822 billion to the government to bring improvements to the people of Panama, a figure nearly equal to what was contributed to Panama during the previous 86 years of US management. All of this laid a foundation of trust in the Panamanians' management of the Canal, which would serve well the cause of any future expansion plans.

At the same time, quietly behind the scenes, the ACP was planning an even bigger step: the massive expansion program that would eventually propel the Canal into a quantum capacity leap in the twenty-first century and beyond.

Expansion Plans Take Root

In early 2001, just a few months after the handover, the ACP launched a series of studies that explored various aspects of what an expansion of the Canal would look like. Knowing that there was no earlier example of how to expand the Canal to build on, the leadership of the ACP realized that they would be breaking brand-new ground in every area. The number of studies undertaken ultimately reached more than 100 in total, costing some $40 million.

On the business side, several reports delved into the Canal's current operating capacity and built forecast models to determine the preliminary requirements for the expansion program. Another ten financial and economic analyses of the cost of the proposed expansion were carried out. Several more studies explored macro and micro the trends of the global maritime market. Others looked at the competitive environment represented in the logistics proposals for multimodal cargo handling.

Moreover, from the engineering perspective, research was conducted as to size of the new locks and the feasibility of the project to deepen and widen the channels of Gatun Lake and the Culebra Cut. Detailed examinations into the measurement of marine currents and aspects of the structures of the hydrographic basin were conducted. Additional studies on the potential impact of the expansion on the flora, fauna, and species living within the area to be intervened were done. Excavations were made to determine the existence of archaeological and paleontological remains in the area where the locks were possibly to be built.

The scale of the research process was enormous. In addition to conducting dozens of research projects themselves—and coordinating all the research projects contracted to outside firms—the team needed to collate all their findings, analyze the data, and translate it into readable and presentable formats. It took dozens of people working around-the-clock for nearly 5 years to make it happen.

Finally, on April 24, 2006, the Board of Directors of the ACP presented to the nation the proposal for the expansion of the Canal through the construction of a third set of locks. In a formal act broadcast throughout the country, President Martín Torrijos Espino received the proposal from the president of the Board of Directors of the Authority, Ricaurte Vásquez Morales. The Administrator and CEO Alberto Alemán Zubieta. The Board expressed the project as necessary, convenient, and economically profitable and ultimately recommended its implementation.

Ricaurte Vásquez highlighted the significance of the project. Alemán Zubieta continued with a well-condensed exposition of the technical and financial aspects of the work. He stressed, to clear up any doubts, that the expansion would be self-financed through the resources and efforts of the Canal and a loan requested from multilateral development banks.

The 55,000 pages of expansion studies carried out by the Canal Authority were then released to the public for the purpose of giving every Panamanian the opportunity to learn every aspect of the project and make an informed decision in the forthcoming referendum. The people of Panama spoke on October 22, 2006, with a 77% vote in favor of the expansion. The future of the Canal was defined.

Starts, Fits, and Success

That year, Quijano was invited to lead the entire expansion project. This stage of his career would be much different than his previous roles. Over the course of the next several years, Quijano would build a new organization that would be dedicated to meeting the needs of the Canal Expansion, including establishing the budget, recruiting qualified personnel, creating the project schedule, preparing specifications for the contracting of more studies, purchasing equipment, constructing central and field offices, and overseeing thousands of contracts, along with many other responsibilities, each running in parallel together! Thirteen months later, on September 3, 2007, with a blast at Cerro Paraíso on the Pacific side, work began on the expansion of the Canal of Panama. On July 15, 2009, Grupo Unidos por el Canal (GUPC) was awarded the contract to design and build the new set of locks, considered the largest and most important aspect of the expansion program.

On July 1, 2011, the permanent concrete pouring began in the Third Set of Locks project; and, between April and June 2013, the entrances were widened and deepened to allow the transit of "Neopanamax" vessels, which could pass through the new Canal locks when completed. In March 2012, as the work progressed and the finish line was coming into view, the Board of Directors of the ACP appointed Quijano to replace Alberto Alemán Zubieta as Administrator and CEO of the Panama Canal upon completion of his second 7-year term. As his deputy administrator, the Board of Directors chose his valued friend, colleague, and great supporter Manuel E. Benítez. Alberto Alemán formally passed the torch to Quijano on September 3, 2012.

As Administrator, Quijano had to fulfill a different role in the framework of the expansion. Ilya Espino de Marotta replaced him as program manager and did an extraordinary job. And, while the scale and responsibility of Quijano's roles during the expansion approached overwhelming, one of the biggest challenges he faced as Administrator was the oversight of so many contractors at the same time. There were almost 4,200 contracts for procurement, works, supplies, consultancies, studies, and equipment, and everything was within the budget estimated in 2006! An example of the challenges faced by Quijano and his team illustrates this:

By the end of 2013, GUPC, which had already completed 65% of the work, threatened to suspend the construction if the ACP did not agree to its request to pay additional costs without following the steps established in the original contract. Tough negotiations began on January 7, but GUPC, far from working on a solution, rejected any initiative, unilaterally increased the figure for additional costs, and maintained its threat to paralyze the work.

As they had throughout the entire project, Quijano and the ACP kept their commitment to act in total transparency out of respect for the Panamanian people who had supported the expansion. On January 21, when GUPC went forward with its threat and stopped work in February, Quijano and the ACP called a press conference to make a detailed account of the events since the end of December 2013. The ACP's position was crystal clear: they would finish the construction with GUPC or without GUPC; and, even more, they already had a "Plan B" in place to make it happen if GUPC did not continue with the work. Both sides dug in to see what would happen next.

Although they were very difficult times for everyone at the Canal and for the country, the ACP stood firm so that the contract was respected and continued to demand the resumption of the works at the rate both parties had originally agreed to. Weeks of tension and uncertainty followed. Neither side budged. Critically, the support of the Panamanian people for the ACP never wavered. It energized Quijano and the ACP to defend their principles.

Still, as the work stoppage continued, Quijano was shocked to see the project in total abandonment, with parked machinery, and the dry February wind passing through the half-finished locks. This scene was very painful. Many sleepless nights followed.

Finally, on February 27, 2014, a conceptual agreement was announced, subject to review and legal signature, which took place just a week and a half later. The parties agreed on a new schedule whose outcome would be the completion of the work by December 2015.

On April 28, 2015, the last of the 16 gates of the new locks were installed on the Pacific side, while, in June, the work entered its final stretch with the beginning of the filling of the two locks: Cocolí, on the Pacific, and Aguas Claras on the Atlantic. The first tests of the new gates were also done. On September 14, 2015, the filling of the new access channel began, which connects the Culebra Cut with the new locks in the Pacific sector; and, on February 5, 2016, the testing of the water recycling basins began.

Finally, on June 26, 2016, at 7:30 am, the container ship "Cosco Shipping Panama" approached the lower chamber of the new Atlantic Agua Clara Locks near Colón. The vessel measured 48.25 m wide and 299.98 m long and had the capacity to transport 9400 containers. It was the largest ship to have ever passed through the Canal in its history. It had originated in Greece and was heading across the Pacific Ocean to South Korea.

More than 20,000 Panamanians gathered at the new Aguas Claras Locks in Colón and 35,000 more at the Cocolí locks, on the Pacific, for the inauguration of the new expanded Canal. The ship stopped in the upper chamber, and there the official photograph was taken: an image as important as that of August 15, 1914, when a solitary steamer—the "SS Ancon"—inaugurated the Canal. On that historic day in 2016, Quijano proudly announced "this is the greatest work that has been done in a century on our soil."

Looking Back

It is curious that history insists on placing human beings from different eras in similar challenges. It certainly was not an easy undertaking in the nineteenth century to start the construction of an interoceanic canal in Panama. Nor was it easy to expand it into the twenty-first century. Quijano and others understood that to expand the interoceanic route was to leverage all of Panama's resources: most importantly its people. Despite the long hours, tense moments, and daring that were required, Quijano never lost faith in his fellow Panamanians.

The expansion's conclusion paved the way for a 63% jump in year-over-year revenue contributed to the nation from the first year of full operation of the Canal expansion. This major undertaking and its successful completion was a reflection of the best of the Panamanian people. Ten of thousands of Panamanians, from tradesmen and technicians to various branches of engineering, the natural sciences, finance and law, and dozens of other disciplines, represented the more 90% of the total workforce that made it all possible. In short, the expansion of the Canal will always be known as a masterpiece of human resolve and a testament to Panamanian leadership and ingenuity.

Chapter 4
The Canal of Panama and the Natural Gas Revolution

Before you become too entranced with gorgeous gadgets and mesmerizing video displays, let me remind you that information is not knowledge, knowledge is not wisdom, and wisdom is not foresight. Each grows out of the other, and we need them all.

—Arthur C. Clarke

Yes, my grandfather worked with Thomas Edison on the electric car, and he sold electric cars at the 1900 World's Fair in Paris.

—Al Jardine, American musician

Formula for success: Rise early. Work hard. Strike oil.

—J. Paul Getty

In retrospect it becomes clear that hindsight is definitely overrated!

—Alfred E. Newman

By nearly every measure, the operation of the Canal since 2000 has been a tremendous success for Panama and the global economy. In fiscal year 2021 (October), a record amount of tonnage passed through the Canal. This was more than a 10% increase over fiscal year 2019, which was prior to the COVID-19 pandemic. Despite massive interruptions in global supply chains resulting from measures in response to the virus, the Canal saw increases in the different kinds of cargo that it handles. 2021 also witnessed the continued growth of the Canal's fastest rising segments: liquid natural gas (LNG), which rose by more than 30% over 2019, and natural gas liquids (NGLs), which rose by more than 20%.[1]

The Canal is uniquely positioned to take full advantage of what has quietly become known as the natural gas revolution. Despite all the constant buzz around renewable energy sources, going green, zero emissions, etc., we are still in the early stages of the Carbon Era, which the world entered during World War I. The

[1] Henry Cardenas P. "El Canal de Panamá registra récord de tonelaje, 10% más que en 2019" *La Prensa* October 28, 2021, https://www.prensa.com/economia/el-canal-de-panama-registra-record-de-tonelaje-10-mas-que-en-2019/ Accessed January 31, 2022.

A. R. Thomas, *The Canal of Panama and Globalization*,
https://doi.org/10.1007/978-3-031-05152-4_4

exponential increase of the production and usage of natural gas in recent years, combined with the expanded Canal, which allows for the larger ships to now transmit the Canal, is proving to be a gamechanger for both the Canal and the global economy. For example, for US LNG exports to East Asia, the distance from the US Gulf to Japan is around 9214 nautical miles, compared with 14,570 nautical miles via the Suez Canal. Assuming a speed of 19.5 knots, the reduced distance can result in savings of around 22 days on a round trip voyage from Panama.

The Natural Gas Revolution: Unforeseen and Very Welcome

A hydrocarbon which shares space with petroleum and coal, natural gas, is quickly becoming *the* way forward to reduce emissions and provide cleaner, higher efficient energy to more of the human population. While politicians and climate activists tend to make the most noise and grab the headlines, it is the capitalists and their actions which tell us so much more about the trendlines. In his 2022 letter to his CEOs, BlackRock Chairman Larry Fink—who has more than $10.5 trillion in assets under management—wrote "traditional fossil fuels like natural gas will play an important role to ensure continuity of affordable energy supplies during the transition"; "any plan that focuses solely on limiting supply and fails to address demand for hydrocarbons will drive up energy prices for those who can least afford it"; and "BlackRock does not pursue divestment from oil and gas companies as a policy."[2]

Interestingly, the same attitude toward natural gas is now prevalent across the European Union. In the Fall of 2021, the UN-sponsored CO26 conference was held in Glasgow. Promoted as "A pivotal moment in the fight against climate change," next to nothing was truly accomplished except some virtue-signaling against carbon by the those who traveled in their private jets to attend. Of course, there was the usual goal setting around the move to a "zero-emission world"—whatever that means—some number of years far into the future. In this case, it was around 2049. After all the predictable posturing, the thousands of attendees fired up their carbon-fueled planes and headed home. A few weeks later, the European Union very quietly announced that natural gas—a dirty hydrocarbon—was now classified as a necessary energy source for the Continent's future. The EU Commission stated, "There is a role for natural gas as a means to facilitate the transition towards a predominantly renewable-based future." This means that natural gas will be classified as a "sustainable investment" going forward.[3] As Robert Bryce so accurately pointed out in 2008—and remains true today:

---

[2] Larry Fink's 2022 Letter to CEOs "The Power of Capitalism" https://www.blackrock.com/corporate/investor-relations/larry-fink-ceo-letter# Accessed January 31, 2022.

[3] EU Commission "EU Taxonomy: Commission begins expert consultations on Complementary Delegated Act covering certain nuclear and gas activities" Press Release, January 1, 2022 https://ec.europa.eu/commission/presscorner/detail/en/ip_22_2 Accessed January 31, 2022.

> *While alternative forms of energy will make minor contributions… they cannot supplant the new global energy paradigm, one in which every type of fossil fuel – crude oil, natural gas, diesel fuel, gasoline, coal, and uranium- gets traded and shipped in an ever more sophisticated global market.*[4]

Like the rest of the world, Europe will not be able to move to a predominantly renewable energy future any time this century. Carbon—and increasingly, natural gas—will dominate the course of our grandchildren's lives. It seems the Europeans are slowly realizing that reality—irrespective of one's wishes—still drives the train. For the Canal, this realization will be a boon to its operations in the coming decades.

American Shale Energy

Not long ago, the United States was planning to import tens of millions of metric tons of liquid natural gas (LNG) each year to meet its own power needs. Now, in one of those unexpected twists than no one predicted, the United States is now producing about the same amount and sending it out to Asia, Europe, and other overseas markets. In 2020, the United States became the third largest LNG exporter in the world—behind only Australia and Qatar. Once the new LNG liquefaction trains, at Sabine Pass and Calcasieu Pass in Louisiana, are operational sometime in 2022, the United States will have the world's largest LNG export capacity. That dramatic shift—from the expectation of the United States being a major natural gas importer to the reality of being a leading producer and exporter—has had a huge impact on the global energy market. The influence on the Canal and globalization cannot be understated.

Ask an average group of people when the smartphone revolution began, and you'll likely get some guesses that it was somewhere around the late 1990s.[5] References to Blackberry's and Palm Pilots would populate the responses: and they'd be partly right. I still miss my Blackberry, as the "press keys" remain much better suited to my fat fingers than touch screens. Work on integrating a mobile telephone with a computer and the Internet had started earlier in that decade and accelerated as the Web became more mainstream. Apple's introduction of the first iPhone in 2007 changed forever the world that would follow. The ease of use—particularly for people with skinny fingers—coupled with the style and look of the iPhone, redrew the boundaries and expanded the possibilities for what was possible when it came to personal communication.

While the iPhone debuted in 2007, the technologies that the smartphone integrated were nothing close to new. The telephone was invented in the mid-nineteenth century. The first cellular call was made in 1973. Cellular phones gained widespread

---

[4] Robert Bryce *Gusher of Lies: The Dangerous Delusions of Energy Independence* (2008, Public Affairs) p. 6.

[5] For a good history of the development of the smartphone see Elizabeth Woyke's *The Smartphone: Anatomy of an Industry* (New Press, 2014).

popularity by the early 1990s. Computers appeared in the first half of the twentieth century. As micro-processing dramatically improved, personal computers were introduced and mass-marketed in the 1980s. The telegraph—a nineteenth-century invention—was the first fully digital communication system. In the 1960s, the US Defense Department contracted to build the ARPANET (Advanced Research Projects Agency Network), which laid the foundation for the Internet. The first message on ARPANET was sent in 1969. By the 1980s, the World Wide Web was under construction. And, by the 1990s, popular usage of the Internet went global. The smartphone integrated all these older technologies into an easier, more accessible, more efficient, and more affordable platform. And, it changed the world.

The integration of old technologies into a new, revolutionary platform can also be observed through the development of American shale energy. In this case, two old processes—drilling and "fracking"—have undergone significant upgrades in recent years. Interestingly, the current mix of horizontal drilling and hydraulic fracturing, and the smartphone, are about the same age. And, like the telephone, computer, and Internet, the technologies used in present-day shale energy extraction have been around a long time.

Human beings were making holes in the ground to gain access to water and salt for thousands of years. Many believe it was first the Chinese in 252 BC who developed drilling techniques to access salt brine. The first wells were effectively large pits that gradually got narrower as they descended to about 300 feet. As the Chinese experimented, they later were able to drill narrower and deeper shafts. Sometimes flames or an explosion would rise from the hole and kill people on the surface. This unknown, invisible, and deadly force was initially thought to be an evil spirit from the underworld. By 100 AD, however, the Chinese had learned that the invisible substance was not en evil spirit. Instead, if harnessed properly, it could be a tremendous source of heat. They identified the holes where the invisible substance came out of the ground, lit the holes, and placed the pots nearby. They could cook with it. This was the first known use of natural gas in history.[6]

Drilling into the Earth for water and salt continued to improve over centuries. In 1126 AD, the first "artesian" well with positive pressure (a flowing water well) was drilled by a group of monks in the French province of Artois.[7] In the early seventeenth century, the "Grenelle Well"—another French artesian water—implemented a dry rotary auger method and reached 1771 feet. It took 8 years.[8] Francis Drake's well in 1859 in Titusville, Pennsylvania, was the first successful commercial venture designed to locate and extract oil. Using cable-assisted tooling, it drilled to 69 feet in about a week.

As oil demand grew, principally as the energy source for lighting, the next few years saw some radical experimentation in drilling and extraction methods. The use

---

[6] Mark Kurlansky *Salt: A World History* (Knopf Canada, 2011), p. 8.

[7] Elias Howard Sellards "Occurrence and Use of Artesian and Other Underground Water" *Issue 89 of Bulletin* (University of Florida Agricultural Experiment Station, 1907), p. 107.

[8] Pierre Hyacinthe Azais *Explanation and History of the Artesian Well of Grenelle* (University of Chicago, 1845), p. 9.

of "Roberts' Torpedoes" became the most popular method. Named after their inventor, Colonel E.A.L. Roberts, a veteran of both the Mexican War and Civil War, the first "torpedoes," which were encased in iron, contained somewhere between 15 and 20 pounds of gun powder. They were then lowered into the well, near to where it was believed the greatest amount of "fracture" of rock would occur once the torpedo was detonated. In November 1866, Roberts was awarded US Patent No. 59,936 for torpedoes. Later versions preferred nitroglycerin to gun powder. The process was as simple as it was successful. Filling the borehole with water provided Roberts his "fluid tamping" to concentrate concussion and more efficiently fracture surrounding oil strata. The technique had an immediate impact—production from some wells increased 1200% within a week of being "shot"—and the Roberts Petroleum Torpedo Company flourished.[9]

Roberts' notion of "fracturing" the subsurface rock to release any trapped organic material was a breakthrough in the long history of human beings making holes in the Earth and extracting resources from them. Still, this was a very dangerous business. As noted by John J. McLaurin in 1896, "A flame or a spark would not explode Nitro-Glycerin readily, but the chap who struck it a hard rap might as well avoid trouble among his heirs by having had his will written and a cigar-box ordered to hold such fragments as his weeping relatives could pick from the surrounding district."[10]

While nitroglycerin remained in use far into the twentieth century, other safer, and more effective, means were being sought to force trapped carbon to the surface.

At this point, it's important to take a step back and recognize that "fracturing"—or "fracking" as it has been popularly labeled in recent years—is a process done for the purpose of getting a specific kind of rock to give up its contents. Fracturing the rock is simply a means to an end. And, human beings have been doing it for more than a century and a half.

As we learned in high-school science class, there are three main types of rocks: sedimentary, metamorphic, and igneous. About 95% of the Earth's crust is made up of either igneous or metamorphic rocks. Only 5% of the Earth's crust contains sedimentary rock. Moreover, there are only three types of sedimentary rocks that can potentially contain usable oil and natural gas. They are shale, sandstone, and limestone. Within each kind of these sedimentary rocks rests the remains of long-dead, carbon-based organisms that fused with grains and mineral particles (also known as sediments) as water ran over them. Because these kinds of rocks are bound together by such small components, they are porous in nature, which means they are full of spaces that energy-rich carbon compounds can settle, later to be liberated in the form of either oil or gas.[11]

---

[9] David A. Waples *The Natural Gas Industry in Appalachia: A History from the First Discovery to the Tapping of the Marcellus Shale, 2nd ed.* (McFarland, 2012), p. 124.

[10] John James McLaurin *Sketches in Crude Oil: Some Accidents and Incidents of the Petroleum Development in All Parts of the Globe* (Publisher: Author, 1896), p. 334.

[11] Darlene R. Stille *Sedimentary Rocks: A Record of Earth's History Exploring* (Capstone, 2008) p. 4.

Shale is a sedimentary rock frequently mentioned as a natural fuel source. This is because of its abundance: more than 40% of all sedimentary rock is shale in its composition. Shale is produced when layers of carbon-rich mud are compressed until they harden into rock that retains those layers. One type of shale contains so much kerogen, the organic solid that gets processed into oil and gas, which is called "oil shale."

Other types of especially porous rocks often form above shale beds, trapping the low-density carbon compounds that may rise through the mud that becomes shale in their spaces. Sandstone is one such rock, created from grains of minerals like quartz bound by other compounds, such as silica. Within sandstone beds such as Alberta, Canada's "tar sands," carbon compounds generally exist in liquid form, as crude oil, that in some cases also releases natural gas when brought to the Earth's surface.

Like sandstone, carbonates are sedimentary rocks commonly found in conjunction with shale. Carbonates, however, are formed largely from remains of marine life, particularly shells and bones, combined with other minerals. Because of this, they are full of calcium and other compounds that lead to their classification: limestones, which contain calcium carbonate, and dolomites, which contain calcium magnesium carbonate.[12] The spaces between their fused fragments are where oil and gas may be found.

To put this all another way, oil and natural gas together make petroleum. Petroleum, which is Latin for *rock oil*, is a fossil fuel, meaning it was made naturally from decaying plant and animal remains. It is a mixture of hundreds of different hydrocarbon molecules containing hydrogen and carbon that exist sometimes as a liquid (crude oil) and sometimes as a vapor (natural gas).

Over hundreds of millions of years, oil and natural gas were formed from the remains of prehistoric plants and animals—that's why they're called fossil fuels. These prehistoric plant and animal remain settled into the seas along with sand, silt, and rocks. As the rocks and silt settled, layer upon layer piled up in rivers, along coastlines, and on the sea bottom trapping the organic material. Without air, the organic layers could not rot away. Over time, increasing pressure and temperature changed the mud, sand, and silt into rock (known as source rock) and slowly "cooked" the organic matter into petroleum. Petroleum is held inside the rock formation, like how a sponge holds water.[13]

The oil and gas that formed in the source rock deep within the Earth moved upward through tiny, connected pore spaces in the rocks. Some seeped out at the Earth's surface. Nonporous rocks or other barriers trapped most of the petroleum hydrocarbons. These underground traps of oil and gas are called reservoirs. Contrary to popular misconception, reservoirs are not underground "lakes" of oil; they are made up of porous and permeable rocks that can hold significant amounts of oil and

---

[12] Ibid., p. 17.

[13] Energy4me.org "Petroleum and Natural Gas" http://energy4me.org/all-about-energy/what-is-energy/energy-sources/petroleum/ Accessed January 2, 2022.

gas within their pore spaces. Some reservoirs are hundreds of feet below the surface, while others are thousands of feet underground.

"Fracking" is the process used to break up, or "fracture", the porous, underground sedimentary rock formations that contain oil and natural gas. Once the source rock is fractured, its contents will migrate to the surface. Over time, human experimentation and tinkering began to move away from the nitroglycerin-based torpedoes of the nineteenth century toward safer and more sustainable fracking methods. On March 17, 1949, a team of petroleum production engineers performed the first commercial application of hydraulic fracturing about 12 miles east of Duncan, Oklahoma. Later that same day, personnel of Halliburton and Stanolind successfully fractured another oil well near Holliday, Texas, using pressurized water as the catalyst. Hydraulic fracturing is a technique in which rock is fractured by a pressurized liquid.

The process involves the high-pressure injection of "fracking fluid" (a kind of gel that is a mix of primarily water, sand, and other proppants suspended with the aid of thickening agents) into a well bore to create cracks in the deep-rock formations through which natural gas, petroleum, and brine would flow more freely. When the hydraulic pressure is removed from the well, small grains of hydraulic fracturing proppants (either sand or aluminum oxide) hold the fractures open. The technique was developed and patented by Stanolind (later known as Pan American Oil Company), and exclusively license was issued to Halliburton.[14] By 1953, all credentialed oil and gas service companies were given access to this new process. Tinkering and experimentation continued as more than one million wells were drilled using this gel-based hydraulic fracturing method.[15]

Still, there were limitations to how much this process could achieve. People within the energy industry knew there was more, probably a lot more, petroleum trapped within sedimentary rock, particularly shale that the current cocktail couldn't access. The questions were: How to get it? And, just as important, how to do it as inexpensively as possible?

In a classic case of American-style creativity, risk-taking, and entrepreneurialism, Nick Steinsberger, a 34-year-old petroleum engineer working for Mitchell Energy, unleashed one of the biggest "open sesames" of the modern era on June 11, 1998. On that day, Steinsberger added massive amounts of injected water to the cocktail, which cracked the shale beneath S.H. Griffin Well #4 in North Texas. A few days later, to the astonishment of everyone, the well was producing more natural gas than could ever be imagined. Steinsberger had figured out how to force shale to give up all its hidden treasure.[16] Nevertheless, Steinsberger's breakthrough wasn't enough to make America's shale energy revolution a reality. To make it possible, significant advances in drilling techniques needed to occur as well.

---

[14] American Oil & Gas Historical Society, "Shooters" – a fracking history", https://aoghs.org/technology/hydraulic-fracturing/ Accessed, January 6, 2022.

[15] Ibid.

[16] Russell Gold *The Boom: How Fracking Ignited the American Energy Revolution and Changed the World* (Simon and Schuster, 2015), p. 115–117.

Horizontal drilling is the process of drilling a well vertically from the surface to a subsurface location just above the target oil or natural gas reservoir (commonly called the "kickoff point"). This process is like the drilling process for a traditional vertical oil or gas well. The difference is that a horizontal well deviates or turns the well bore horizontally to intersect the oil and natural gas reservoir at a specific entry point.

The result is a better pathway for oil and natural gas is created to reach the well bore. In a very basic sense, a horizontal lateral is like a drainage ditch a farmer might use to drain water from their fields; horizontal drilling has two key benefits. First, the flow of oil and natural gas into the well bore is dramatically increased. In a traditional vertical well, approximately 50 feet of the well bore is open to capture oil and natural gas. A horizontal lateral can go a mile or farther into the reservoir rock formation, exposing more oil and natural gas reserves to the well bore. Additionally, and this is the big point here, horizontal drilling has led to reducing the overall footprint of oil and natural gas activity. As the example in the following graphic shows, this horizontal well produces the energy of 32 oil or natural gas wells. Prior to horizontal drilling technology, you would have had to drill 32 wells in the area to get the same energy production as 1 horizontal well.[17] The economies of scale that horizontal drilling represent are stunning.

Traditional Vertical Well Spacing:
32 Separate Padsites Needed For 32 Wells.

Idealized Horizontal Well Spacing:
1 Padsite Yields Up To 32 Wells.

[17] Ohio Oil and Gas Association "Ohio Shale Plays" http://www.ooga.org/?page=OhioShalePlays. Accessed January 22, 2022.

When drilling into a hydrocarbon-bearing formation 100 feet thick, vertical drilling would allow an operator to contact 100 feet of rock, which would reduce the potential recovery to whatever oil or gas might flow into that length of pipe. Horizontal drilling now allows these same operators to drill and set pipe for a mile or more horizontally through this same rock formation. The driller is now contacting and fracturing 5200 feet of rock rather than 100 feet, which exponentially multiplies expected well recovery rates and provides massive economies of scale.[18] The technology employed is so advanced and exacting that drillers today can hit a target at the end of a drill string that is 10,000 feet vertical with a mile-long horizontal section that is no more than a few inches in diameter.[19]

In the United States over the past 16 years, the precision and scale of hydraulic fracturing and horizontal drilling have combined with unique American characteristics to give the nation's shale energy revolution its full weight. Carbon-containing shale rock is in many different regions around the world. It is not exclusively within the United States. The fracturing and drilling techniques now being used are widely known to anybody with an Internet connection. Still, the shale energy revolution remains almost an exclusively American affair. This is not to say that other nations are not exploring—or already exploiting—this natural resource. The United Kingdom, Argentina, Bulgaria, and Romania, among others, are looking to ramp up their domestic shale energy industries. Yet, it is in America where the results have been truly staggering. The reason for the tremendous success in the United States can be attributed to some moving parts that have coalesced around shale energy to make it all possible.

First, of course, is geology. In this respect, nature has been tremendously kind to the United States. The conditions needed to unfold over hundreds of millions of years to generate carbon-producing shale rock that occurred in many places across America's geology. Luck seemingly has its privileges. Next is the distinctive American way that property rights and mineral rights are viewed. In every other nation in the world, the owner or leaser does not hold any mineral rights attached to any piece of private property. Instead, the national government controls them. Any decision on how to access those minerals is a government decision at the highest levels. In the United States, the opposite is the case. Mineral rights are privately held and can be passed to the new property owner or held separately. This has meant that those who own mineral rights are able to allow energy exploration companies to do their work.

Doing the work is no easy matter. America's long history of energy development throughout the Carbon Era has created generations of the world's top geologists, petroleum engineers, geophysicists, surveyors, pipeline layers, drillers, welders, and journeymen. The collective learning in these fields over decades has given America all the labor she's needed to make the shale energy revolution come to life.

---

[18] David Blackmon "Horizontal Drilling: A Technological Marvel Ignored", *Forbes*, January 28, 2013, https://www.forbes.com/sites/davidblackmon/2013/01/28/horizontal-drilling-a-technological-marvel-ignored/#1aec4e326f11 Accessed January 6, 2022.

[19] Ibid.

Much of the requisite capital necessary to fund America's shale energy revolution (estimated by many to already be more than $1.5 trillion since 2007) emanates from the world's most sophisticated financial system. While the US financial system has taken a public beating in recent years—some of it well-deserved—there is nowhere in the world where the allocation of capital occurs with greater efficiency and speed. The ability for shale energy entrepreneurs to align with sources of capital is one of the least reported—and most important—stories on financial development over the last decade.

The energy infrastructure that was already in place in America prior to the shale energy revolution provided the backbone to its recent stunning growth. By the 1990s, there were nearly a million miles of gas and oil pipeline across the country. Let me repeat that: a million miles of pipeline, or two round trips to the Moon. Refining and storage facilities were well developed. The new infrastructure that has been constructed since 2007 enhances an already well-developed energy system.

We can look back at the last 16 years or so with complete hindsight. Even now, it needs to be remembered that it was entrepreneurs, financers, and risk-takers who, without the benefit of knowing where it would go, got onboard the shale energy train. They made so much of it possible. This very American style of bold—some might say reckless—entrepreneurship is so often desired by the rest of the world yet rarely found outside America's borders.

Finally, at any moment over the past many years, the government could have stepped in and changed the pace or direction. At the national level, both the W. Bush and Obama Administrations maintained an arm's-length distance from what was unfolding. Driven by the greater need to secure more domestic energy supply, the Federal government did nothing of consequence to stop the development of American shale energy. When confronted with challenges from opponents of fossil fuels and those concerned about their increasing use, both Presidents opted to use the federalism provision and outsource the final decision to the States themselves.

As a result, America's shale energy revolution has been driven much more by what happens at the local and state level than in Washington. This devolution of political power is something that doesn't get enough attention by today's Beltway-obsessed culture. The experimentation that marks American entrepreneurialism is also manifested by the tinkering which takes place every day across America's 50 states and its thousands of local governments.

All of this—technological advance, luck, and unique societal attributes—have aligned to bring us to this point. Every day, American energy firms and entrepreneurs continue to explore ways to reduce inefficiencies, increase their profits, and consistently produce more energy. American investors—and, now increasingly, foreign ones—calculate and recalculate their returns on capital, seeking to maximize the best position possible. American political leaders and civil servants at all levels of government pursue solutions to best manage this change for their constituents. It is not hyperbole to say that we are living at an inflection point. We are at the beginning stages of a new ascendancy of American energy. The United States has become once again the largest energy-producing nation on Earth. The implications derived from America's shale energy revolution are now beginning to reveal themselves.

Natural Gas Liquids (NGLs)

During the exploration and production process, both oil and natural gas migrate to the surface. Petroleum and gas are then separated. At processing plants, natural gas can be broken down into liquids, the principal ones being ethane, butane, propane, heptanes, hexane, and pentanes. Each of these serves as the critical foundations for so many indispensable aspects of our lives.

Ethane is mainly used to produce ethylene, which is then used by the petrochemical industry to produce a range of intermediate products, most of which are converted into plastics. Ethane can also be used directly as a fuel for power generation, either on its own or blended with natural gas.

Butane has many applications, including as a liquid fuel, a propellant for aerosol sprays, and a base for production of other petrochemicals. Although some normal butane is used as a fuel for lighters, most of it is blended into gasoline, especially during the cooler months.

Pentane is a natural gasoline (also known as pentanes plus) that can be blended into the fuels used in internal combustion engines, particularly motor gasoline. In the United States, natural gasoline is added to fuel ethanol as a denaturant to make the ethanol undrinkable, which is required by law.

Propane is used primarily as a heat source. Most of the propane consumed in the United States is used as a fuel, generally in areas where the supply of natural gas is limited or not available. This use is highly seasonal, with the largest consumption occurring in the fall and winter months. Propane sold as a fuel for the consumer market is generally defined as HD-5, which contains a minimum of 90% propane by volume, with small quantities of other hydrocarbon gases. HD-10, which contains up to 10% propylene, is the accepted standard for propane in California.

There are two general market categories for propane: consumer (primarily as fuel) and non-consumer (primarily for nonfuel or feedstock uses). There are four major consumer uses of propane: in homes, for space heating and water heating, for cooking, for drying clothes, and for fueling gas fireplaces, barbecue grills, and backup electrical generators; on farms, for heating livestock housing and greenhouses, for drying crops, for pest and weed control, and for powering farm equipment and irrigation pumps; in businesses and industry, to power fork lifts, electric welders, and other equipment; and as a fuel for on-road internal combustion engine vehicles such as cars, school busses, or delivery vans and non-road vehicles such as tractors and lawn mowers.[20]

The non-consumer market for propane is the petrochemical industry. The primary use of propane in the petrochemical industry is as a feedstock, along with ethane and naphtha, in petrochemical crackers to produce ethylene, propylene, and

---

[20] U.S. Department of Energy "Natural Gas Liquids Primer with a Focus on the Appalachian Region" December 2017, p. 2–4. https://www.energy.gov/sites/prod/files/2017/12/f46/NGL%20Primer.pdf Accessed January 24, 2022.

other olefins. Propylene and the other olefins may be converted into a variety of products, mostly plastics and resins and glues, solvents, and coatings.

Heptanes are widely used in the manufacturing of paints, sealants, and pharmaceuticals. While *hexane* can be found in chemicals that are used to make shoes, leather products, and roofing, these chemicals can also be used to extract cooking oils (such as canola oil or soy oil) from seeds, for cleansing and degreasing a variety of items, and in textile manufacturing.

Quality is something that is taken for granted until it can't be found. The past practice of offshoring NGL and petrochemical production from the United States to lower-cost markets has often come at the expense of quality and product safety. Numerous incidents involving poor-quality NGLs made in China have blared across the headlines in recent years. Products from tainted pet food that killed and sickened thousands of animals to toys that were covered in lead-based paint and to personal care products like toothpaste that were deemed poisonous had many international firms reevaluating their original decision to go to China in the first place. Now those same firms have options whether to do business in China at all.

The Rise of US Shale Energy Exports

The transformation of America from an increasingly dependent *importer* of energy to a growing *exporter* is one of the more recent developments of the shale energy revolution. Since 1953, America's surging economy demanded more energy than the nation could produce. More and more energy imports were needed to make up America's deficit. The strains and vulnerabilities of decreasing domestic energy security revealed themselves in the 1970s and remained potent until the arrival of the shale energy surge. Today, looking forward, the United States has once again returned to the position of a net exporter of energy

The central focus of US shale energy exports is predominantly on the LNG product of methane, which is used in heating and cooking as well as electricity generation and other industrial applications. While not as dramatic the expansion of LNG, the export of natural gas liquids (NGLs) from the United States more than doubled in the period 2015–2020.[21]

For transport on the ocean, shale gas is converted to liquid form for ease and safety of non-pressurized storage. The liquids are shipped around the world in specially constructed massive seagoing vessels of which almost the entire global fleet can transit the Canal.

The global liquid gas market has changed exponentially in the past 20 years. As late as the early 2000s, the United States was constructing multibillion-dollar facilities along the Gulf Coast that would process natural gas *imports*, looking to make

[21] U.S. Energy Information Administration "Export *of Petroleum and Liquids 2015–2020*" https://www.eia.gov/dnav/pet/PET_MOVE_EXP_A_EPL2_EEX_MBBLPD_A.htm Accessed February 5, 2022.

up for America's energy deficit. Today, the opposite is the case. Massive capital investment is being plowed into *export* infrastructure across the region: thanks to dramatic growth in US domestic natural gas production.

Exports from the Unites States have taken place in two waves. The first was typified by "Brownfield" conversion projects: taking preexisting *import* terminals and adding liquefaction capability and other necessary infrastructure improvements, so that they can now *export*. Existing US import terminal owners/operators have added liquefaction/export capabilities as a means of adapting to the rapid growth in the global natural gas market in the short term. However, as Kathleen Eisbrenner, the founder and CEO of NextDecade, a Houston-based LNG development company focused on export projects, points out, "there is only a finite number of existing import terminals that can and will be converted to export facilities, and that number is not enough to satisfy future demand."[22]

According to Eisbrenner, the demand that made the first wave viable has continued to grow and that is leading to the second wave of US exports. These are "Greenfield" projects, developed purposefully from the ground up to meet the anticipated continued, growing, and new global demand and prevent an impending global natural gas supply shortage. New Greenfield projects "have a number of benefits, including made-for-purpose design, and its associated cost and production efficiencies, as well as the ability for developers to select advantageous site locations with proximity and access to gas supply, among others."[23]

Of course, the United States is not the only place seeking to expand its natural gas exports. Other nations such as Australia and Qatar are ramping up their production as well, under the assumption that demand from importing nations will continue to rise. In 2018, China overtook South Korea and Japan to become the world's largest natural gas importer. Those three nations constitute about 65% of global natural gas consumption. Today, much of the rise in demand from China comes from that nation's desire to reduce coal burning for household heating and replace it with much cleaner natural gas. In November 2017, at the Chinese Communist Party Congress, Premier Xi Jinping made a cleaner environment a top national priority. Chinese imports have risen almost 70% since then. If you've ever been to a Chinese city, the impact from all the coal burning reminds one why natural gas is a far better option.

As natural gas is a global commodity, its cost and availability ultimately determine the quantity sold. For US newcomers, this will mean fierce competition from existing exporters who have historically dominated this business. In addition, the increased complexity of doing cross-border trade, the challenges that arise from both physical and cultural distance, and the higher costs to the enterprise that global business requires will all test the mettle of US exporters in the coming years.

---

[22] Matthew V. Veazey "Views from the Crest of LNG's Second Wave: NextDecade's Kathleen Eisbrenner" *Rigzone.com* November 01, 2017, https://www.rigzone.com/news/views_from_the_crest_of_lngs_second_wave_nextdecades_kathleen_eisbrenner-01-nov-2017-152299-article/ accessed January 28, 2022.

[23] Ibid.

It seems, at least in the short term, that the stars may be aligned for the United States as it pursues growth in LNG exports. "LNG is going to be very important to North America overall and the United States in particular," says John Baguley, Chief Operating Officer LNG Limited (LNGL), which is pursuing export terminal projects in Louisiana and Nova Scotia. "Even more so, U.S. LNG is going to be extremely important to the world energy market."[24] Calling the United States a "stable, long-term, reliable" supplier of highly competitively priced LNG, Baguley said that it enjoys a unique position among LNG-exporting countries. "It is not possible today to identify another place in the world that provides this critical combination of price and certainty."[25]

The Canal and American Shale Energy

While the shale energy revolution was developing in the United States, Panama was expanding the capacity of the Canal under the leadership of Jorge Quijano and the ACP. It would be too much to say that the Panamanians predicted the advent of American shale energy. As mentioned before, no one saw it coming. Instead, we can say that the Panamanians put themselves squarely in a position to benefit. If luck is when opportunity meets preparation, then we'll call the Panamanians lucky.

On July 25, 2016, the first transit through the Canal of a liquefied natural gas (LNG) carrier took place. Using the new locks, the Shell-chartered Maran Gas Apollonia, measuring 289 m by 45 m, arrived from the Sabine Pass LNG Terminal on the US Gulf Coast. In public statements at the time, ACP Administrator Quijano said:

> *The transit of the first LNG vessel through the new Panama Canal locks is a milestone in the waterway's history. The LNG trade will greatly benefit from the Expansion, and we look forward to welcoming even more LNG vessels through our great waterway. This transit marks the beginning of a new era that will result in cleaner and lower cost energy for the world.*

The Canal can now accommodate 90% of the world's LNG tankers, which has had a major impact on global LNG flows, including offering numerous benefits and options to shippers. As mentioned, the Canal allows vessels departing the US East and Gulf Coasts for Asia to enjoy significant reductions in voyage times: making US gas deliveries to major Asian importers very competitive.

Vessels departing the US Gulf Coast for the West Coast of South America similarly experience generous time savings. In addition, LNG ships from production plants in Trinidad and Tobago heading to Chile where LNG is re-gasified and

[24] Matthew V. Veazey "Views from the Crest of LNG's Second Wave: LNGL's John Baguley" *Rigzone.com* Nov 2, 2017, https://www.rigzone.com/news/views_from_the_crest_of_lngs_second_wave_lngls_john_baguley-02-nov-2017-152322-article/. Accessed January 28, 2022.

[25] Ibid.

distributed for energy-producing purposes save 6 days in transit time compared to the historic route through the Magellan Straits around Cape Horn.

Couldn't This All Just Be Hype?

President Obama observed in his 2012 State of the Union Address "We have a supply of natural gas that can last America nearly one hundred years." When the President of the United States says something like this in such a setting, it appears to be definitive. It is only an estimate.

Estimates of future reserves are at best marginal attempts to quantify how much energy would be recoverable using current technology and practices. What is rarely taken into account—because of the level of difficulty of seeing into the future—is what the final cost of extraction will be. As energy prices fluctuate regularly, today's potential windfall can easily become tomorrow's loser. To date, energy companies have only tapped a tiny fraction of the known shale formations in the country, so data points on recoveries, gas quality, flow rates, and other metrics remain few.[26]

When America's shale energy revolution broke out, interest rates and the costs of capital were abnormally low—and remained so for many years. Government stimulus and subsequent central bank interest rate manipulation in the wake of the global financial crisis forced capital into more risky areas in pursuit of better returns: areas where investment may have not normally flowed. Had interest rates been appreciably higher in the period from 2008 to 2017, America's shale energy industry may not have received the incredible levels of investment that made the revolution possible in the first place. Going forward, a rise in the cost of capital—coupled with continued low returns on investment and the rise in extraction costs—could turn down the spigot of investors and further put pressure on prices to rise.

Regarding demand, there is a fundamental assumption that a surging global middle class enjoined with expanding prosperity will naturally require more and more hydrocarbon energy production. At a recent energy conference in October 2021, Professor Vaclav Smil, one of the world's top energy experts, pointed out that the world still gets 83% of its energy from fossil fuels, with the range from 99% for the Middle East to 91% for Australia, 87% for China, and 83% for the United States. Germany has spent the last 20 years turning itself "green," yet it still relies on fossil fuels for 78% of its energy. Smil further noted that since the first global climate meeting in 1992, the world's dependence on fossil fuels has only fallen from 87% to 83%. In absolute terms, humans are using more fossil fuels today. All the investment in renewable energy has resulted in only meeting some of the incremental demand growth of recent years.[27]

---

[26] Charles R. Morris *Comeback: America's New Economic Boom* (Public Affairs, 2013) p. 36.

[27] Comments by Professor Vaclav Smil at the Credit Suisse-sponsored "APAC ESG Conference 2021: Powering the transition" October 20, 2021.

Smil told his audience, "Now I am told in the next 30 years by 2050, we are going to go from 83% to zero. That strains one's imagination. We are burning more than 10 billion tons of fossil fuels and we are dependent, in every facet of existence."[28] He pointed to ammonia-based nitrogen fertilizer, which is made from natural gas. Without it, we could probably feed only half the world's population. Human civilization is dependent on four pillars: steel, ammonia, cement, and plastics. They all require lots of fossil fuels. There are no easy replacements.

On the issue of climate change, Smil has no problem. He says it was acknowledged in 1860. In his view, the problem is the energy transition and the push by organizations such as the International Energy Agency, whose policy prescriptions he believes to be out of alignment. "We are in the very early stages of the transition from fossil fuels to something else," he says. "It took us 100 years to go from wood to 50% coal, 100 years to go from zero oil to about 40% oil. It has taken us so far about 70 years to go from zero gas to about 25% gas. These transitions are always unfolding, always at their own sweet pace. This could be accelerated, but within reason. You can't say 'by 2030 or by 2035' – it doesn't work that way."[29]

Technology is pointed to as the vehicle to speed up the transition, but Smil is skeptical. He pointed to the Norwegian experience with electrifying container shipping. "The Norwegians put into operation the first electric container ship just this year with 120 containers. It goes about 30 nautical miles. The biggest container ships in the world carry 24,000 containers, can easily go 13,000 nautical miles." Shipping is under the gun to go "clean" but with no technical or economic solution. Furthermore, we have been developing electric vehicles for about 20 years, and now we have seven million on the road, competing with 1.2 billion internal combustion engine vehicles. The natural gas revolution is still in its early stages. Given that, the Canal is in a strong position to take full advantage going forward.[30]

[28] Ibid.

[29] Ibid.

[30] Ibid.

Chapter 5
Macro-trends Impacting the Future of the Canal and Globalization

Science has not yet mastered prophecy. We predict too much for the next year and yet far too little for the next 10.

— Neil Armstrong

It's tough to make predictions, especially about the future.

— Yogi Berra

Any astronomer can predict with absolute accuracy just where every star in the universe will be at 11.30 tonight. He can make no such prediction about his teenage daughter.

— James Truslow Adams

Follow the trendlines, not the headlines.

— Anonymous

The remaining portion of this book explores what might lie ahead for the Canal and globalization. Only a fool would try to lay out hypotheses, make inferences, and draw conclusions about the future of these two incredibly complex and interrelated themes. I proceed.

Looking into the Future

In the practice of strategic management, discussions abound concerning what comes next. It is one thing to understand both how we got here and where we are. Those are the jobs of historians, academics, and journalists. For the decision-makers of an organization, however, a whole other level of thinking is needed, which considers where we might go and what is needed to get us there. This is the principal reason that CEOs make the big bucks. Among so many responsibilities, it is ultimately their job to figure out what will be happening next. And, then, determine how to best position their organization to take advantage of any new opportunities that are presented, as well as to protect it from changes in the operating environment that could cause harm: a formidable task indeed.

A. R. Thomas, *The Canal of Panama and Globalization*,
https://doi.org/10.1007/978-3-031-05152-4_5

In this chapter, some of the principal Macro-trends that are influencing globalization, and therefore much of the future of the Canal, are laid out. These are elements that cannot be controlled or influenced by the ACP. Nonetheless, they will significantly shape the operating environment in which the Canal exists.

A Caveat: The COVID-19 Pandemic

This analysis was conducted during the first half of 2022. At that moment, a once-in-a-century global pandemic was entering its third year. COVID-19 arrived from China sometime in late 2019 and quickly spread around the world in a matter of weeks. It can be argued that the pandemic which followed has been the single most "global" event in human history. Meaning, the virus and the many public health responses to it have touched almost every person on the planet in one way or another. One could consider that the World Wars were every bit as pervasive to the global population. I would disagree. For many regular folks, particularly in large parts of Latin America, Africa, and South Asia, the Wars were only news clips from far-away places.

COVID, on the other hand, has impacted much more of humanity. For a few, the impact from death and disease has been severe. For most everyone else, continued fear and uncertainty, along with significant disruptions to economic and social daily life, have been the biggest jolts. At one point, in the Spring of 2020, nearly 6 billion people—out of a total world population of 7.8 billion—were in one way or another locked down by government decree to stop the spread of the virus. Many lockdowns continued long after this initial surge.

In Panama, for example, a near total quarantine of the population lasted from early March 2020 to late October. While the economy "reopened" in November 2020, additional selective lockdowns were put in place in December 2020 and lasted until April 2021. This was a similar story in many places around the world.

The extreme government measures in response to the arrival of COVID-19 were a first in human history: the intentional closing of large parts of the economy and society to control the spread of a respiratory virus. The impacts of these decisions will have ramifications for decades to come. Since human interventions had never been done before at this scale, we have no way of knowing their final affects. The bomb went off, and we are just beginning to experience the shockwaves.

In Panama and across most of Latin America, children had not been in school for 2 full years. If they had been learning at all, it was through television and the Internet. While we can speculate as to what this means to the present and future well-being of these kids and their societies, it will take a long time to fully understand the impact.

Economies around the world are still reeling from the fallout of the interventions. Tens of millions of small and medium-size businesses were destroyed overnight. Huge swaths of commercial and retail spaces sit empty, with no prospects about what their future holds. Tens of millions have fallen back into extreme poverty.

Larger companies quickly filled the gap and got much, much bigger. Wealth became more concentrated in the hands of an ever-smaller group of elites. The future implications remain unknown. Whole industries—like business travel, live entertainment, and construction—are a fraction of what they once were. Will they ever recover to their pre-pandemic levels? No one knows.

Dishearteningly, the pandemic is nowhere near to being over. The Omicron variant, which appeared on the scene in November 2021, spread itself around the world in less than 2 months. The third highly infectious variant to quickly "go global" (the original Wuhan and Delta strains being the other two), Omicron probably made more human beings ill at the same time than in any period since the Spanish Flu pandemic of 1918. Unlike the previous strains, when Omicron showed up nearly half of humanity had received at least one COVID shot. Many individuals later followed up and got their second dose, while others more sought out boosters. What is clear now as the pandemic enters its third year is that the jabs are not what they were promised to be. Most people who took them believed they would be protected from getting COVID-19. That is not the case. In many countries, many of the sickest from Omicron were vaccinated. It was also assumed that if vaccinated, one would not transmit the virus to others. We now know transmission of the virus readily takes place irrespective of vaccine status.

The shots were administered in the middle of a pandemic with the virus circulating all around. This was a first in history. We know that after a vaccine is administered, it takes several weeks for the vaccine to reach its optimal effect. Because the virus is present everywhere, there is a good chance that it will infect people whose immunity, induced by the vaccine, is still in the process of being strengthened. The virus can therefore multiply and immediately use this opportunity to adapt to the immune pressure that vaccinated people exert on its infectious power.

Vaccinated people thus act as a kind of battlefield for the virus where only the strongest (aka the more infectious) variants survive. If many people in the population have been vaccinated, mutual contamination will cause the number of surviving viruses to increase rapidly and further spread the virus. This will be more likely as the variant is less well recognized by the antibodies that the vaccine induces in the population.

Serious concerns remain that deploying "leaky" vaccines will continue to lead to increasingly higher infectious variants. If, during a pandemic of such an easily mutating virus, a vaccine is used that is unable to prevent the virus from infecting people and then spreading, the virus now has the opportunity to select a variant that is increasingly unaffected by the vaccine. This is a perfect case study of Darwin's evolution by natural selection in action. In hindsight, the notion that humanity was going to vaccinate itself out of the pandemic of a rapidly mutating respiratory virus was a flawed concept.

While no one can predict what might happen next, we need to pay ever closer attention to the virus' evolution. Pandemic fatigue has expectedly set in around the world after more than 2 years of fits, starts, mandates, and the like. People are ready to get back to a degree of normalcy and want to view COVID-19 merely as another endemic virus: like the seasonal flu.

However, just because we want something to happen doesn't make it so. We learned this as children. You simply can't wish things away. A pandemic is a global evolutionary event that is highly unpredictable. The Omicron variant could be the last highly contagious variant. What follows might well be less contagious and dangerous than what went before. That would be awesome news.

At the same time, due to the immune pressure placed on the virus by the unprecedented human interventions, an even more contagious and lethal variant might well be selected by Nature. Given the poor track record of the "experts" throughout the pandemic to anticipate what comes next, we should be prepared for all contingencies. Remember: Nature always gets to bat last.

As we explore the Macro-trends potentially impacting the future of the Canal and globalization, it is sensible to look at them through the lens of COVID-19. The virus is not going to disappear. Given that it has also been found in many other mammals, reservoirs for the virus will always exist to keep it alive. The question here is: what are the most likely paths for the virus and humanity going forward? For purposes of coherence, each Macro-trend will be evaluated within (three) different potential trajectories of COVID-19:

1. *The Best-Case Scenario*: This occurs when the virus recedes to endemic status sometime in 2022–2023. The virus looks like the annual flu: dangerous for a few while relatively straightforward to manage. At the endemic level, the virus is much more treatable and better understood. Human beings—like they always do—improvise, adapt, and overcome: this time to return to a degree of pre-pandemic normalcy while co-existing with a diminished virus.
2. *The Middle-Case Scenario*: This finds highly contagious variants like Delta and Omicron continuing to flare up and cause widespread sickness and disease. This is the muddling scenario, where we continue to play whack-a-mole, and ride the waves of an ever-evolving active virus until we figure out how to best manage it with new or existing therapeutics and antivirals. It is the Michael Corleone trap: "Just when I thought I was out, they pull me back in." This extends the pandemic into 2024 or beyond.
3. *The Worst-Case Scenario*: This is the stuff of nightmares. A more infectious and dangerous variant is naturally selected. The new strain breaks through all attempts to reduce severe disease and death. The result is widespread serious illness and the death of 10s or 100s of millions of human beings, including young and healthy people. This is where Nature resets the pandemic to Day Zero—and it starts all again.

The Macro-trends were in place before the pandemic hit. Some of them have been altered by COVID-19. Others were exacerbated. This section will lay out the principal Macro-trends that will likely impact the future of the Canal and globalization along with their possible trajectories relevant to COVID-19.

Macro-trend: A Plunge in the Human Population

Politicians, journalists, and environmental activists—among others—have convinced huge swaths of humanity that the current global population of 7.8 billion will simply swell by another 2–3 billion *homos sapiens* during this century. They couldn't be more wrong in one sentence. Such silly thinking has led to whole industries of fearmongering about more and more human beings laying waste to the planet. The threat of climate change is just the latest in a long line of hysteria around an out-of-control human population that cannot sustain itself here on Earth.

Way prior to the arrival of COVID-19, the biggest story—which was almost never reported in the popular press—was the unfolding precipitous decline in the human population. As it stands today, we will never make it to eight billion. Soon enough, and irrespective of the pandemic, humanity is on the verge of the most significant alteration of our time on the planet. Until very recently, humanity fought—sometimes on the razor's edge—to simply survive and perpetuate the species. Now, for the first time in history, human beings are self-selecting to reduce their numbers on planet Earth.

The reasons are not too difficult to understand. Because of the widespread availability of effective contraception, women have had the power to control their reproduction for several generations now. As the world has become much more urbanized in recent decades, children are no longer assets that can readily help in the fields. Instead, children raised in cities—at least on the balance sheet—are financial liabilities that require huge levels of investment to sustain. As any parent knows, kids are expensive. Further, the surging pool of empowered women who gravitate to cities are more apt to focus on their personal development first, and seek a mate later, if they so choose. For those women who *do* find a mate *and* desire to have a child, the average age of procreation and marriage has almost doubled in most parts of the world. Because of these factors, women all over the world are ultimately having far fewer children: if they do at all.

It all adds up to the fact we human beings are not making enough babies to replace those who die every year. And, don't think this is just a "rich world" phenomenon. It is happening everywhere—and at a pace faster than most people realize. The global population is soon to shrink and is headed down a one-way street.[1]

Once unleashed, there is no turning back. The implications of this are almost beyond comprehension. From alterations of global trade and consumer patterns to shifts in energy demand to the impact on the environment to security and defense and to almost everything else, this is the biggest story around.

For the ACP and anyone who does international business, trying to figure this one out will present a monumental challenge. Organizations which are today exploring global population decline and what it means for themselves and their

[1] A must-read book on the subject of global population decline is Darrell Bricker and John Ibbitson *Empty Planet: The Shock of Global Population Decline* (2019, Signal).

stakeholders should stay far ahead of their competitors. Prioritizing this as a top organizational goal could well become a competitive advantage.

COVID-19 best case	COVID-19 middle case	COVID-19 worst case
Birth rates have plummeted even faster around the world since the onset of the pandemic. The quicker the ending of the crisis, the more likely a reduction in the pace of falling global birth rates would occur.	A continuation of the current situation into the next few years would exacerbate falling birth rates—and accelerate the rate of the plunge.	In this situation, we would expect the falling rate of births to be off the charts. Add in the damage by significant early deaths from a deadlier variant(s), the decline of the human population would be precipitous.

Macro-trend: Increasing Government Involvement in Every Aspect of Life

The role of government in people's daily lives has been getting more involved over time. For Americans and Europeans, this has been the case for much of the postwar era. The levels of government spending and new legislation introduced each year seem to surpass the previous ones. In large swaths of the developing world, the government has been even more immersed.

The arrival of COVID-19 gave government officials around the world an opportunity to ingratiate themselves in ways never-before imagined. The word "unprecedented" was thrown around a lot at the outset of the lockdowns and implementation of the countermeasures. What was most unprecedented of all was governments' intervention in areas that were normally off limits to bureaucrats. A new power—one to restrict basic human contact and gathering—was used with full force in much of the world. This was truly revolutionary.

As the pandemic has unfolded, it appears government will keep this item on the menu going forward. It is now part of the growing list that governments can choose from when they believe it warranted. The extent to which government expansion continues with regard to the three possible COVID-19 scenarios follows:

COVID-19 best case	COVID-19 middle case	COVID-19 worst case
As the virus moves to its endemic phase, governments relax the most stringent restrictions while always keeping the option for reinstatement open. Many governmental support programs to relieve the financial impact to businesses and individuals will be removed.	Governments continue to intervene when they believe the situation is approaching a potentially critical level. Increased government reach will ebb and flow in conjunction with the waves of viral spread over time. The longer the pandemic continues, many of the governmental support programs introduced to ease the burden of the interventions will have become part of the normal package of public benefits. At the end, we will have found that government involvement will have significantly and permanently increased.	A variant usurpation of all human interventions that leads to more death will force governments to respond once again with versions of massive lockdowns. This time much more force will be applied to assure compliance. Widespread civil unrest and violence will result. To curb its spread, large injections of cash into the hands of the public will follow (effectively bribing people to stay home) further raising record government debt levels.

Macro-trend: Expanded Government Intervention in the Economy

Well before the pandemic, governments intervened in the economy in any number of ways. Political economy—the intersection of business with government—played a larger role year after year. Government spending as a percentage of GDP has risen in almost every country over the past 75 years—so much, in fact, that nearly every government has spent far more beyond its means. National debt levels, which were rising prior to the pandemic, have skyrocketed since. Increased government spending on health care, vaccines, personal protective equipment, etc. will continue for years to come. Subsidies to populations in the form of reduced utility bills (water, electric, cable bills, etc.), as well as direct cash payments, enhanced unemployment benefits, and the suspension of loan payments, are some of the more common government interventions. It is estimated that COVID-19 has added somewhere around $40 trillion to the debts of nations.

Across the world, government's reach into the economy hit unfathomable heights when—in the name of public health—huge swaths of legitimate business activity overnight was reclassified as "dangerous" or "non-essential." Hundreds of millions of people lost their businesses or jobs in an instant. This was particularly the case in the developing world, where upward of half of all economic activity occurs in the informal sector. Much of this selection by government as to what is "good" or "bad" economic activity continues up till today. Rather than market forces and individual choice determining the behavior of consumers, governments have stepped into that role as well: coercing consumers to change their buying habits and preferences.

COVID-19 best case	COVID-19 middle case	COVID-19 worst case
The endemic phase would allow governments to focus on the benefits of economic growth once again. Restrictions on certain economic activities will continue to be erased, and the feeling of a pre-pandemic economy will be more realized.	In some places, governments would continue to provide widespread support to sectors and individuals that are still being impacted by the viral waves, keeping them afloat with hopes things will subside one day. In others, government will insist that certain sectors simply remain too dangerous to fully reopen and displaced workers will have to move on. Permanent closures follow.	Governments quickly return to the "essential" vs. "non-essential" classification of the private sector. In this scenario, more pressure than ever would be placed on "non-essential" activities to remain completely closed, while the "essentials" would receive more government support.

Macro-trend: The Emerging Global Debt Crisis

The pandemic gave cover to politicians and central bankers to do extraordinary things when the global economy was shuttered in 2020. First, government spending levels went vertical. In the name of "fighting COVID-19," the United States in 2020 and 2021 added more than $8 trillion—or nearly 25% of the total—to its national debt. That is about the same as the combined GDP of Japan and Germany! The United States certainly wasn't alone. China added more than 30% to its national debt. Across the European Union, the pandemic pushed national debts more than 13% higher on average, while the United Kingdom saw an 18% increase.

The problem of increasing national debt is not a significant one so long as the cost of financing that debt is acceptable. Prior to the pandemic, global inflation and interest rates were both low by historical standards. In response to the lockdowns, the major central banks, including the US Federal Reserve, European Central Bank, Bank of England, and Bank of Japan, all raced to cut interest rates lower, much lower, to effectively below zero. As the economy reopened, demand surged and inflation reentered the picture. As a result, the pressure on central bankers to raise interest rates is building.

Whenever the Federal Reserve substantially raises interest rates, the fallout is immediate and widespread. Nearly 70% of all global currencies by volume are linked to the US dollar. This makes Fed policy much more influential than that of other central banks. Further, nine-tenths of all global commerce outside of the Eurozone is conducted in dollars. And, every global commodity that is traded—i.e., oil, natural gas, coal, rice, wheat, cotton, etc.—and much of steel, ammonia, concrete, and plastic are done in dollars. The value of the dollar touches everyone and everything on the planet. A change in its value resonates globally.

COVID-19 best case	COVID-19 middle case	COVID-19 worst case
A quick shift to an endemic state would provide a good amount of breathing room to both governments and the Fed to better manage increased debt levels and deal with any interest rate adjustments. This more methodical approach—without the pressure of the pandemic—would provide for increased predictability for central bankers, policy-makers, investors, and the private sector.	The continuance of highly infectious viral waves (i.e., Delta and Omicron) could delay any adjustments to government spending around COVID-19, while pushing needed interest rate considerations down the road. These delays could make the debt crisis much worse than had action been taken earlier to deal with it.	The emergence of a truly deadly variant will force governments to intervene with massive spending once again. All bets off would be as to the consequences from this scenario, except to say they wouldn't be good.

Macro-trend: Nations Are Becoming More Insular

Globalization is the opening up of local economies to the influences of foreign players. It allows travelers, capital, firms, knowledge, products, and services from other countries to have relatively easy access to a nation's domestic markets. The reciprocity of allowing others to do the same is the foundation of the modern capitalist system established at Bretton Woods. Except for North Korea, Cuba, and Venezuela, every nation on Earth has bought in to this notion.

Then the pandemic hit. Immediately, international borders were shut to nonresidents. Nations scrambled to find personal protective equipment for their own citizens at the expense of their neighboring countries. Other key necessities were hoarded, and export controls were reintroduced in many countries. Supply chains frayed and, in some cases, ground to a halt. As time unfolded, nations started to hoard natural gas, oil, and coal when they could. Globalization was pushed back. Churchill's reminder that "Nations do not have friends they have only interests" was self-evident.

COVID-19 best case	COVID-19 middle case	COVID-19 worst case
A quick retreat of the virus would provide national leaders with the confidence to actively adjust their international connections. This won't stop the trend to insularity. It would, however, slow it down.	The continued emergence of highly contagious variants would make it much more difficult for nations to remove the many measures put in place to restrict international travel, tourism, and trade. The longer the status quo continues, the more difficult it would be to return to pre-pandemic levels of openness.	The appearance of a "super variant" would put the focus once again on local and national efforts to protect populations at all costs. This would be the unleashing of a wave of selfish nationalism that would be like nothing any of us have ever seen.

Macro-trend: Rising Global Energy Shortages and Higher Prices

The breathless campaign for renewables to reduce and eventually replace hydrocarbons is running out of steam. Lazy pronouncements wax endlessly about being "carbon neutral" or achieving "zero emissions" by such and such date. In the real world, vacuous statements like these reduce any credibility the speaker may have left. The "electrification" of all things sounds great to uninformed zealots who just despise hydrocarbons. Yet, reality is never far away. In the US alone, "electrification" would mean the addition of more than 500,000 miles of high-voltage transmission lines! Already, more and more local governments across all 50 states are prohibiting any new lines from ever being introduced. Even the Europeans have finally thrown in the towel and announced that natural gas is a vital energy source going forward. More revealing, in early 2022 Germany announced it is accelerating the construction of several new LNG import terminals to stave off an energy catastrophe. This is a 180-degree switch from when Germany loudly proclaimed that it was embarking on a 100% renewable energy goal by the early 2020s.

A more mature understanding of the real world poses a challenge. For example, the shale energy revolution in its current form may be slowing down—and a lot quicker than we would hope. Legitimate concerns are emerging that show the number of "sweet spots" for frackers might be getting smaller in number. In other words, given the current technology and investment levels, most easy wells will be tapped within the next few years.

In the future, access to the harder-to-get shale will cost much more to produce—and that will require large amounts of new capital investment. That could only occur when energy prices are high enough to justify investor risk. This is a tough proposition for producers. Given the past weak outcomes from the shale energy revolution for investors, they could be too skittish to jump back in. Instead, what we may possibly see going forward is the easier path. To stay profitable, producers would intentionally maintain high energy prices over a longer period as they seek to squeeze out all they can from the easier and cheaper "sweet spots." They would do this by reducing supply.

COVID-19 best case	COVID-19 middle case	COVID-19 worst case
The risks posed by rising energy prices and shortages are made much more manageable for governments and firms if it occurs within the context of a waning pandemic. The ability to hedge future prices and better predict production and market trends are enhanced by a more stable environment.	The muddling scenario of the virus makes acting upon energy shortages and price rises much more fraught with difficulty and uncertainty.	If the world falls back into extreme lockdowns to battle a super variant, the future of energy prices and production would be impossible to determine. One thing would be certain: many nations would hoard domestic energy for themselves, reducing exports and impacting nations that are import dependent.

Macro-trend: A Significant Realignment of US Foreign Policy

What forms the natural tendencies of American foreign policy? Is it the isolationism of the late nineteenth and early twentieth centuries? Is it the Wilsonian view of American engagement in the twentieth century that led to the creation of the Bretton Woods system? Is it a desire on the part of elites like Henry Luce to spread American ideals around the world? Or, is it the goal to enrich American firms and investors by tapping into new markets around the world? As with any complicated question, there are many elements that constitute the answer. Nevertheless, it is clear the post-World War II international system is beginning to wind down. The pullback of the United States from the guarantees that have underpinned the system is already underway.

Many might think America's floundering commitment is the result of Donald Trump's election in November 2016. This is too narrowly focused. Most recently, the American people have chosen three Presidents who campaigned on disentangling the United States from its post-World War II assurances.

Barack Obama's notion of America "leading from behind" became a fundamental pillar of his second administration's foreign policy. As a candidate and President, Obama railed against US entanglements and nation building. Even George W. Bush, who might be best remembered for leading the adventures into Iraq, Afghanistan, and beyond, was elected in 2000 on a platform of disengagement from the rest of the world. The 9/11 attacks radically changed Bush's views and likely would have altered Al Gore's had he been President. Of course, Bush was also confronted with the very serious threat of America's growing dependency on foreign sources of energy to sustain the global system it created. For Obama, once American shale energy entered the equation, he was able to return to his instincts and seek to limit America's involvement in foreign affairs. If anything, Trump's election was simply the logical progression of America's reevaluation of Bretton Woods. As has been observed, "W. Bush abused America's allies, Obama ignored them, and Trump insulted them." The first years of the Biden Administration is no different as exemplified by the Afghanistan pullout and the reluctance to put American "boots on the ground" in Ukraine.

A fundamental reality of the Bretton Woods commitments that the United States laid out to the allies—and then everyone else—is the lack of involvement of the American people in its creation. The Bretton Woods Conference was held in July 1944, four months before a Presidential election and a month after the allied landings at D-Day. The attention of the American people and many of their elected representatives was clearly elsewhere. Remembering that Woodrow Wilson's appeal to the US Senate for passage of his 14-Points was rejected, the Roosevelt Administration took a far different course. When given its chance during World War II to create "The American Century," the Roosevelt Administration didn't bother with constitutional requirements under Article I. They simply ignored Congress' sole authority to approve foreign treaties and agreements. Instead, they just did it.

Over time, the reality of Bretton Woods melded into a kind of *fait accompli*, where America was the creator and sustainer of the new international system. No one really challenged the creation of Bretton Woods because no one—except for a few key elites—was even aware that it had been created in the first place. By the time the war ended and people learned of its existence, Bretton Woods was already too far down the road.

Foreign policy—and support for the Bretton Woods system—remained the purview of a small American elite across governmental agencies, academe, industry, and the military for generations. These unelected folks guided incoming Presidents in the "ways of the world"—and argued for the consensus that the Bretton Woods system must always be supported. The only American presidents with any kind of international relations experience after World War II were Dwight Eisenhower and George H.W. Bush, both of whom deeply supported the Bretton Woods system and America's role in maintaining it. The others leaned heavily on entrenched foreign policy elites in the Pentagon, State Department, CIA, multinational corporations, and universities for guidance and direction.

Paradoxically, the one nation that has come up short in enjoying so many of the tremendous benefits of the American-led Bretton Woods system is the United States itself. The United States is overwhelmingly a domestic-focused economy and always has been. Today, only about 18% of all US GDP is tied to international trade, with around half of that being specialized energy imports, which are declining fast. This is consistent with the past 150 years of history.

Moreover, concerns about burgeoning entitlement costs—READ Medicare and Medicaid—as the baby boomers continue to exit the workplace find more and more Americans rightly worried about ballooning deficits and obligations to their fellow citizens—and themselves. Trade agreements that were positioned to the American people as fundamental to continued prosperity began to lose credibility with voters of all stripes as factories shuttered and millions of jobs were outsourced overseas.

The major party candidates in 2016—Trump and Hilary Clinton—both rejected America joining the Trans-Pacific Partnership, which had taken over a decade to negotiate and was birthed in the United States. Despite his toned-down rhetoric, Joe Biden seems to be following his predecessors "less is better" approach when it comes to American foreign policy. The withdraw from Afghanistan—as poorly executed and embarrassing as it was—still finds large support among most Americans: who are just glad that the country's longest war is finally over. In Ukraine, the US appears ready to fight to the last Ukrainian.

In short, Americans across the political spectrum have been asking for more than 20 years, "What is our return-on-investment for the trillions we have spent to build and maintain the global capitalist system?" Answers are hard to find. There are, of course, domestic benefits to America's engagement with the global economy, yet they are not as profound as many believe and quite difficult to articulate for the supporters of an activist role. This internal debate within the United States about the future of America's role in the world will only intensify in coming years. Its implications will be massive for humanity. Equally important, while it is clear the Americans are trying to figure out what makes the best sense for *them* going forward, the rest of the world is not standing idly by and waiting for answers. It can't afford to. In short, the world has already been preparing for the post Bretton Woods era for a while now.

In the immediate period after the Cold War ended, the United States accounted for around 60% of total world expenditures on arms and weapons. As it became clear that the Americans were re-evaluating the country's commitment to Bretton Woods, other nations began to bolster their military spending. Today, the Americans account for less than 40% of all global military spending, and it keeps falling. In 2021, annual US military spending was lower than it was in 2010. Despite the pandemic, non-US global military spending has increased by nearly 15% over the last two years.

The trendline is inexorably moving towards a world where more nations are spending ever-larger amounts of resources to build up their military capabilities. Moreover, the actions of many nations confirm that they believe rising global insecurity is at hand. When that happens, war and rumors of war return to the strategic calculus.

COVID-19 best case	COVID-19 middle case	COVID-19 worst case
The pandemic has already further soured the American people on globalization. Calls are coming from all corners to bring critical manufacturing and services back to the United States. China is blamed for the pandemic by a growing number of Americans. Increasingly, the United States' populationsees the world more as a nuisance or a threat than a benefit.	Any continuance of the pandemic would further strain the view most Americans hold about their nation's global commitments. Elections at the national level would find credible candidates from both parties aggressively de-emphasizing the Bretton Woods system and promising to end it once and for all.	This would lead to "America First" on steroids. Bretton Woods would be set a path toward extinction much quicker than might be imagined.

Macro-trend: Significant Repositioning of Global Supply Chains

One of the most important results from the Bretton Woods era was the expansion of global supply chains to more and more nations. In Southeast Asia, first, defeated Japan, and later South Korea, Singapore, Taiwan, the Philippines, Malaysia, Thailand, Indonesia, and even Vietnam and China—who each fought bloody wars against the Americans after Bretton Woods—took full advantage to make their peoples live better. They have all built societies that would have been unimaginable just a couple of decades prior. The former Soviet republics of Central and Eastern Europe have sprinted ahead with much of the same vigor as their Southeast Asian counterparts. The quality of life has dramatically improved in these nations as well since they joined in the 1990s.

The expansion of global supply chains to more and more corners of the globe brought with it a deeper level of integration which is rarely appreciated. It is not simply about leveraging lower-cost materials, labor, and manufacturing capacity to make products that drive supply chain expansion. These are a big part of it, yes. Nevertheless, the deeper integration results from the package of knowledge sharing, personal interaction, and innovation that is a product of, in Matt Ridley's eloquent phrase, "Ideas having sex."[2] Once something is learned or experienced, it cannot be taken away. Despite the best attempts by lawyers with their non-competes and NDAs, new information and knowledge cannot be stored away in some hermetically sealed bubble forever. Like water, ideas and exchange eventually find a way out.

When Romanian employees at the Timken plant outside of Bucharest go to work each day, they are not just merely producing quality steel products. They are also interacting with a world thousands of miles away. They are seeing and experiencing the ways Americans do things. They are learning about preferences and differences in the places where their steel products are sold. The American managers, too, get quite the education. They see the ways Romanian technicians approach a given

[2] Matt Ridley *The Rational Optimist: How Prosperity Evolves* (2011, Harper).

problem and how they react when confronted with a new challenge. This is what has made globalization such an enriching experience for humankind. It allows us to learn from one another on so many different levels.

One of the many tragedies from the harsh governmental interventions implemented to "control" the pandemic is the destruction of so many small and medium-sized enterprises (SMEs) around the world. SMEs do more than make money for their owners. They provide far higher levels of employment for workers than the biggest global firms. SMEs are also great sources of innovation for new processes, products, and services. SMEs are much more active in their local communities as well. All this- and more- makes SMEs vital for the sustainability of the global middle class and the prosperity it brings. Government action in the name of "flattening the curve" destroyed many SMEs. Those that have been able to survive are often just barely hanging on.

Conversely, the biggest corporations benefitted immensely from the lockdowns and other follow-on measures. The largest supermarket chains, pharmacies, online distributors, do-it-yourself stores, big box retailers, etc. all captured greater market share throughout the first 2 years of the pandemic. Most of this "growth" was government-sponsored and came at the expense of SMEs.

At the same time, global supply chains first almost shutdown completely and then, gradually, reopened, only to discover that significant and long-lasting weaknesses had emerged. Everyone seemingly has a story about how long it now takes to get something that was once so easy and simple to acquire. Just ask the auto manufacturers and their dealers how the computer chip problem is going. To deal with these newfound problems in securing critical components, many SMEs simply did not have the resources to locate new suppliers or absorb exorbitant price increases. The bigger companies did—and were able to use their power to get even larger. Today, and looking forward, the global supply chain challenge does not appear to be going away anytime soon. The biggest firms are seeing this and significantly realigning their supply chains to meet their current and future needs. This is altering the international business landscape in a profound way.

Prior to China's emergence as a global manufacturing center in the 1990s, many US and European firms were embracing offshoring. In the 1980s General Electric under Jack Welch famously relocated several back-office functions to India. However, the conventional wisdom in government, academia, and much of industry was that companies chose to close their costly domestic operations in favor of better prospects and profits in other countries. While it was certainly true that US and European companies were *pulled* overseas by the allure of potential profits and cheap labor, the vast majority were also being *pushed* overseas by something that was much more proximate to the domestic industrial structure than the desire for new markets, lower labor costs, or greater efficiencies in sourcing: the Western world's dysfunctional distribution system. And, although its impact was ubiquitous, the clear connection of this force to the surge in offshoring went largely unnoticed.

It was not corporate avarice that drove a good deal of manufacturing out of the United States. Nor was it the desire for the cheapest price on the part of consumers. What forced thousands of companies to close US and West Europeans operations and lay off workers was an imbalance in the sales and distribution model that has evolved over the past four decades. Distribution has been turned on its head as distributors have wrested control of the strategic prerogatives of manufacturers to capture a disproportionate share of the value of the supplying company's products. Mega-Distributors ended up profiting at the expense of their vendors, and manufacturers earned little or nothing on the sale of their own products. As a result of this phenomenon, US and Western European companies compulsively embraced offshoring not so much because of their internally generated goals and objectives but rather as a necessary response to the demands of sheer corporate survival.[3]

However, the chase for the cheapest input costs hit a brick wall prior to the pandemic. Rising costs—particularly in China—made offshoring there an expensive and increasingly riskier proposition. Significant increases in wages as well as real fears over continued intellectual property theft and poor quality control eventually offset any savings advantages from offshore manufacturing. The rise of "America First" under President Trump and the prospects of a drawn-out trade war gave further impetuous for reshoring. By 2019, for example, both HP and Dell had shifted much of their laptop production out of China. Sony split for Thailand. GoPro left China for Mexico. Under Armour moved out of China in favor of the Philippines. Nike quietly transferred much of its production in China to other facilities in Africa and Asia. Korean electronics giants Samsung and LG both shuttered significant Chinese operations and reshored back to their home country.

The global supply chain disruptions which grew out of the pandemic interventions found the reshoring trendline solidifying. Driven by the need of being as close as possible to their end users, companies further ramped up the realignment. After 25 years in Shenzhen, Stanley Black Decker relocated much of its China-based operations to Fort Worth, Texas, in 2021. Toymaker Hasbro culled half of its Chinese production because of shipping concerns. Microchip maker Intel recently announced new manufacturing facilities in Phoenix and Columbus, Ohio, replacing their Chinese plants.

COVID-19 best case	COVID-19 middle case	COVID-19 worst case
The realignment trend is inexorable. However, the pace of the trend will depend much on the pace of the pandemic. A quick move to the endemic phase would find business leaders being much more deliberate in their supply chain evaluations and selection processes.	A continued re-flaring of highly contagious variants would likely accelerate the tempo of alignment decisions. This would be fostered by the continued supply chain crisis that the pandemic exacerbates.	In this scenario, companies would likely embrace a "damn the torpedoes" approach: meaning whatever they can get home as quickly as possible they would embrace, irrespective of short-term implications like costs. Corporate survival would rule the day.

[3]Andrew R. Thomas & Timothy J. Wilkinson "The Outsourcing Compulsion: How the colonization of American manufacturing by distributors has pushed U.S. companies overseas" *MIT Sloan Management Review* October 1, 2006.

Macro-trend: The Coming Implosion of China

During the 1990s, I witnessed firsthand a slice of China's rise from an isolated, poor country to a major player on the world stage. At the beginning of that decade, more than two-thirds of all Chinese lived in extreme poverty. Twenty-five years later, it was less than 5%.

I remember my first visit to Shanghai. The welcome at the old, dilapidated airport gave depressing a bad name. In the middle of winter, there was no heat, little lighting, and few working facilities to be found. The luggage was unloaded from the plane by a horde of workers and hand carried to the baggage claim area, where it was dutifully placed onto the broken carousel for collection. The hour long queue at immigration was bested by the additional hour-and-a-half waiting for one's suitcases to arrive. On the island surrounded by the kaput carousel, there was on display a locally produced $150 motor scooter, which the attached sign proudly proclaimed as "The best of Chinese engineering!" I was in the motorcycle business and knew the make well. I wouldn't have paid $2 for that piece of junk.

Some years later, my arrival into Shanghai at the sparkling new $2 billion Pudong International Airport got me through immigration in a matter of minutes. The carousels were already spitting out my luggage prior to having entered the baggage claim area. On the island surrounded by the fastest baggage retrieval system in the world was a brand-new luxury Mercedes sedan built in China. It read "The best of Chinese and German engineering!" What a difference a few years can make...

How was China able to do this all so quickly? As Peter Zeihan points out, it was the Americans and Bretton Woods:

> The core problem is that it was not the Chinese who created the environment that made all of contemporary China possible. That was the Americans… The Americans eliminated the powers who had been preying on China for centuries. In granting freedom of the seas to all, the Americans gave the Chinese access to external finance, technology, resources, and markets… In gaining access to the American market, a capital-starved, technology-starved, calorie starved country was able to get all the inputs required to develop, as well as have place to send its manufactured goods.[4]

In other words, if it wasn't for the guarantees afforded by the Americans under the Bretton Woods order, China's miraculous transformation likely would never have happened. Now that those guarantees are winding down, so, too, will the Chinese "miracle".

Internally, over the last four decades, China had every opportunity to build the kind of sustainable institutions that the Japanese, Koreans, and others did. This would have allowed China's society to develop the needed flexibility to manage significant change. Instead the Chinese squandered it all.

As Carl Minzer details, China's reform era has ended. Core factors that characterized it during the 1990s and early 2000s—political stability, ideological

---

[4] Peter Zeihan *Disunited Nations: The Scramble for Power in an Ungoverned World* (2020, Harper Collins) pp. 101–102.

openness, and rapid economic growth—are each unraveling. Since then, a frozen political system has fueled both the rise of entrenched interests within the Communist Party itself and the systematic underdevelopment of institutions of governance among state and society at large. Economic cleavages have widened. Social unrest has worsened. Ideological polarization has deepened. Rather than addressing these looming problems, China's leaders have progressively cannibalized institutional norms and practices that once formed the bedrock of the regime's stability in the reform era.[5] Simply put, while America pulls back on the outside, China insides are crumbling at the same time.

As China's international prestige and its ability to influence external events wanes, more and more domestic pressure is building up. The unaccountable elites who run the Chinese Communist Party have already shown they will do whatever it takes to stay in power, including starving to death tens of millions of their fellow countrymen (The Great Leap Forward), purging all credible institutions of the educated and enlightened (The Cultural Revolution), murdering their own children and their friends when they got out of line (Tiananmen Square), discrediting capitalism (which is currently happening under Premiere-for-Life Xi), and committing genocide against any minority groups who get in the way (Tibetans, Uyghurs, et al.)

No longer able to bribe their urban supporters and the 800 million Chinese who still earn less than $2.50 per day with the hope of returning to double-digit economic growth rates, the leaders of the CCP have firmly changed course. The reform period of the early twenty-first century is now over in China. Liberalization of both society and the economy, along with the new legal institutions designed to support these changes, is all long gone. In its place is a cult of personality rooted in propaganda that feeds a twisted, dystopian view of their leaders to the nation. Legitimate dissent is nonexistent. Adaptive change is now nearly impossible. It won't hold. It never does.

In late 2021, these tremendous weaknesses could be seen in what had become a huge crisis: massively ramping up the production and import of coal to solve the energy crunch the country's increasingly unsustainable economy was facing. Old coal mines were being rapidly brought back into production, and output was being ramped up at existing ones. China continues to scour the globe for coal, knowing the next winter is always just six months away.[6]

China rushed to import coal from North Korea, according to a UN panel of experts responsible for monitoring sanctions on the North on behalf of the Security Council, in violation of international sanctions. The panel obtained satellite images of Chinese coastguard vessels looking on while coal was transferred from North Korean vessels to Chinese-flagged ships.

China's energy crisis was likely its worst in more than two decades. Half of the country's provinces were rationing electricity, factories have closed, and there are

[5] Carl Minzer *End of an Era: How China's Authoritarian Revival is Undermining Its Rise* (2018, Oxford University Press) p. 1–5.

[6] Ibid.

regular blackouts. There are also reports that China is once again bringing in coal from Australia, which would be embarrassing after the country banned Australian imports following a call to investigate into the origins of COVID-19.[7]

If all the above wasn't enough, China is set to experience one of the largest falls in any country's population in the coming decades. Depending how it plays out, China will most likely lose between 350 and 600 million of its citizens by 2100. The bottom number is the current population of the United States. The top number reflects 40% of the entire Chinese population just simply disappearing. Irrespective of the final number of China's population loss, it is almost unfathomable to understand what this will mean.

As China begins to run out of everything that is critical for a stable society-people, transparent institutions, cheap domestic credit, foreign direct investment, energy, food, water, etc., history will again return to the Middle Kingdom. About every century or so, China has a revolution. We are nearly 80 years from the last one. The fractures leading to the next revolution are already forming. Moreover, at this writing, China has implemented its most extreme and widespread COVID-19 lockdowns since the start of the pandemic.

COVID-19 best case	COVID-19 middle case	COVID-19 worst case
China's fall will occur irrespective of the future course of the pandemic. A quick move to endemic might make the landing a bit softer, albeit still inevitable.	A few more years of the pandemic and the current "Zero COVID" policy would only accelerate the coming implosion of China.	The emergence of a far worse variant could put such pressure on China that it would fall upon itself faster than one could imagine.

Each of the above macro-trends are poised to directly impact the future of globalization and, therefore, the Canal of Panama. As the trajectory of the pandemic still remains uncertain, it is best to consider the potential paths it might take within the context of the macro-trends. The next chapter will explore much more proximate elements impacting the Canal.

[7] Ibid.

Chapter 6
Managing Growth, Opportunties, and Challenges for the Canal of Panama

Another flaw in the human character is that everybody wants to build- and nobody wants to do maintenance.

— Kurt Vonnegut

When the well's dry, we know the worth of water.

— Benjamin Franklin

If you don't know history, then you don't know anything. You are a leaf that doesn't know it is part of a tree.

— Michael Crichton

What, me worry?

— Alfred E. Newman

A visit to IPL Group next to the Colon Free Zone is quite instructive about what is right when it comes to Panama as a multimodal global transport hub. A full-service logistics service provider, IPL Group offers a complete portfolio ranging from international transportation, storage and inventory control, sales management, order fulfillment, value-added services, customs, and local deliveries throughout Latin America. With more than 200,000 square feet of physical plant, IPL leverages many of the commercial strengths of Panama for its clients across the fashion, technology, spare parts, e-commerce, retail, and manufacturing sectors.

One of those strengths is the Colon Free Zone. Founded in 1948, it is the largest free trade zone in the Western Hemisphere. The Colon Free Zone is dedicated to re-exporting a wide variety of merchandise that first enters Panama and then is reshipped across Latin America. The Free Zone is located on the Atlantic side, near the entrance to the Canal within both the city and province of Colón. Portobelo, site of the famous trade fairs during the Spanish colonial era, is also located within Colon province, about 20 miles northeast of the Free Zone. Like the Canal, the Colon Free Zone operates as an autonomous entity outside of local government control.

Further, Panama's strategic location for global commerce has been boosted in recent years by the expanded Canal and an enhanced integrated transport

A. R. Thomas, *The Canal of Panama and Globalization*,
https://doi.org/10.1007/978-3-031-05152-4_6

infrastructure. New cargo-handling facilities and a second terminal have been added to Tocumen International Airport, which is the air cargo and passenger hub of Latin America. Significant improvements have also been made to the transcontinental Panama Railroad. A third bridge across the Canal on the Atlantic side was finished just a few years ago. Work is expected to begin shortly on a fourth bridge on the Pacific side, which will parallel a rail tunnel under the Canal.

Moreover, Panama is one of the most digitally connected places on the planet for global firms. International fiber optic networks crisscross the Isthmus: from both oceans and running in every direction. These bundles of cables allow companies to have a nearly unlimited set of options when it comes to accessing reliable, super high-speed connectivity. Organizations like IPL Group can seamlessly link IT systems with their clients and vendors anywhere in the world without interruption.

For global trade, seasonality is a major factor in determining human resource allocation. The Christmas season brings a surge, while the post-Christmas period produces a natural slowdown. The long history of the Colon Free Zone has created a local workforce that is as competent as they are flexible. Firms such as IPL are easily able to make the needed staffing transitions that inevitably occur between the busy and less-busy times.[1]

Yet, below the surface, there do exist some significant challenges to Panama and the Canal that need to be addressed. Globalization is fickle. I doubt many traders at the height of the Portobelo Fairs in the sixteenth and seventeenth centuries would have imagined Panama's future decline into a backwater that lasted nearly 150 years: a place where the Isthmus lingered until the building of the Railroad. It happened before; and, history—while not apt to precisely repeat itself—does often echo.

An inventory of strengths and weaknesses allows us to see where improvements can be made and what challenges to be on the lookout for. These are generally more internally focused and provide a kind of map for the senior leadership. Strengths and weaknesses are also more malleable than the Macro-trends. Meaning, managers can reallocate existing resources or find new ones to leverage the strengths as well as reduce the risks posed by the weaknesses.

Strengths of the Canal

The Lynchpin of an Integrated Global Transportation Network

Panama is located at the heart of the Americas, which is home to nearly a billion people and over $30 trillion of GDP. This represents one-seventh of all humanity with more than 35% of its total wealth. The country is nearly without rivals as to the amount of options it can offer global firms looking to establish operations there: a

[1] In February 2022, the folks at IPL were incredibly gracious to allow me to visit their facility, ask many questions, and provide a tour of the surrounding facilities of the Colon Free Zone.

fully functioning and expanded Canal that can handle almost all the world's commercial vessels, access to the world's two largest and most important oceans, and reliable and direct air cargo and passenger service to much of the Western Hemisphere and beyond.

One of the best ways to know you are doing a good job is when your best clients want to do more business with you. In February 2022, AP Moller Maersk Group announced it was going to open its new Latin American headquarters in Panama. At the press conference announcing the new investment, Robbert Jan Van Trooijen, President of Maersk Latin America, reminded everyone in attendance that his company and Panama share a long history. Maersk is the largest user of the Canal, the Railroad, as well as the ports on both the Pacific and Atlantic sides.

A Strong Culture of Maintenance

It is their fortune that the Panamanians who run the Canal inherited a culture of maintenance from the Americans. They picked up the ball and have been doing a great job running with it ever since. This is a unique and beneficial situation for the day-to-day operations of the Canal and its many stakeholders. As described earlier, the highly aggressive natural environment in Panama will pretty much lay ruin to anything that is not properly maintained. And, with respect to my fellow Panamanians, in many areas outside of the Canal, the approach toward maintenance is suboptimal.

A Leading Reputation for Being a Great Place to Work

The Canal is regularly chosen as one of the best places to work across Central America. Most recently, in 2021, the ACP was once again named as the "Most Admired Workplace" in Panama by both its workers and the country.[2] Internal support from the workforce comes from many areas, including higher than average wages and an atmosphere that has historically supported employee safety, growth, and goal attainment. Moreover, the leadership of the ACP over the past two decades has successfully built into the Canal's workforce the idea that they are doing something greater than just a job each day: they are working for the present and future of the entire nation. This is not mere HR dribble nor sentimentality. Panamanians are

---

[2] The 2021 recognition of ACP was from a regional study conducted by the consulting firm Skaleno Advisory. Further details were published in Roberto Fonseca "Las Empresas Más Admiradas de Centroamérica 2021: cuáles son y cómo es su vision" *E & N* January 18, 2022. https://www.estrategiaynegocios.net/especiales/admirados/1509716-458/las-empresas-m%C3%A1s-admiradas-de-centroam%C3%A9rica-2021-cu%C3%A1les-son-y-c%C3%B3mo-es accessed February 4,2022

fiercely nationalistic and rightly proud of their country and its accomplishments. No athlete there would ever consider taking a knee or making a protest during the playing of the national anthem. Although it doesn't take much to remind the Panamanian workforce of the Canal's importance to their families and fellow citizens, the senior management team consistently makes this point well. All of this combines to make for an incredibly loyal workforce and a place where many Panamanians dream to work one day.

A History of Strong Profitability

Around 80–90% of the Canal's revenue comes from the tolls that it charges the ships who cross between the two oceans. The employees of the Canal work hard every day to deliver value to its *clients*: the shipping companies who pay to use the route. By doing a quality job serving the shipping industry, managing costs, performing regular maintenance and upgrades, etc., the Canal seeks to maximize revenues for its *customer*: the Panamanian people.

At the end of each fiscal year (October), a press conference is held, and the current head of the ACP presents one of those big checks that you used to see at golf tournaments to the current President of the country. The check represents the amount of the earnings from the Canal each year—minus expenses—that will be transferred to the treasury of the nation. On December 16, 2021, the annual ceremony was held, and it was announced that $2,080,629,685 would be sent to the government from the ACP. Since 2000, the total amount of profits transferred from the Canal to the State has been nearly $20 billion. This amount is already exponentially more than the total amount returned to the US Treasury over the 80 years the Americans managed the Canal.

A Highly Responsive and Effective Management Team

Even before the formal transfer of the Canal, the Panamanians were much more aggressive and innovative when it came to maximizing existing revenue streams, developing new ones, implementing new technologies, and managing shifts within the operational environment. The first elements of this included widening the Culebra Cut, which allows for two-way Panamax traffic, an upgrade to the original electromechanical lock machinery with new hydraulic systems, a new fleet of the locomotives which are used to maintain transiting vessels in position while in the locks, and an increase in the number of tow boats which guide ships on the approaches to the locks. All of this began under Panamanian leadership prior to the official handover.

Since then, the Panamanians have instituted a much more dynamic toll and scheduling system, which provides flexibility to its consumers and has increased revenue over the long term. As discussed previously, the expansion of the Canal with the addition of the new Neopanamax lanes has already been a great success. At the same time, the Canal has been a leader in the integration of new IT systems across multiple platforms to support and serve its many stakeholders: both internally and externally. All this adds up to new records of tonnage, transits, and revenues nearly each year.

A Stable Domestic Political Scene

Everybody complains about politicians. Panamanians are no exception. Nonetheless, just a quick glance around Panama's neighborhood reveals how good they have it. Venezuela is a mess and operates more as a narco-state than anything else. Many of its best and brightest can be found living outside the country. In fact, the Venezuela diaspora is so widely dispersed that the country's famous cuisine can be found in almost every major metropolitan area across the United States, Europe, and the Americas. Colombia has made big strides in recent years reducing insecurity and political violence. Still, the influence of the drug cartels remains strong. It always seems Colombia is one bad event away from sliding back into the abyss.

In Central America, Panama is politically an outlier. So is next door Costa Rica. Both nations pride themselves on being above the fray when it comes to Latin America's highly charged politics. The remainder of the region is fitful and politically unstable. Nicaragua ebbs and flows between dictatorship and democracy. Honduras, El Salvador, and Guatemala are some of the largest exporters of their citizens to the north.

Since the American "invasion" and removal of Noriega in 1989, Panama has held six presidential elections. None of the results were contested; and, no acts of widespread fraud or blatant manipulation were ever recorded. More importantly, no political party has repeated the next cycle. Meaning, after each 5-year presidential term, which is the maximum a president can serve under the Constitution, the Panamanians have each time elected new leadership from a different party. In other words, the Panama electorate is less ideologically driven by party loyalty than other democracies. About 30% of the electorate are swing voters—and they make politicians battle it out every 5 years for their support. This ensures a robust debate around national issues and a relatively high degree of accountability not found in more rigid countries. Having this assuredness of political continuity and stability enhances the operating environment for the Canal and its stakeholders.

The Canal's Full Participation in the Shale Energy Revolution

The fortuitous timing of the expanded Canal with the shale energy revolution could not have been better. As US exports of LNG and NGLs to Asia—and beyond—will continue to rise, the Canal will handle ever-larger numbers of energy-related transits. The impact on the Canal's bottom line has already been extraordinary. Not to rest on its laurels, Panama and the US firm Energy Transfer signed a Memorandum of Understanding (MOU) in July 2021. The MOU laid out the details of a joint study to assess the feasibility of a proposed Trans-Panama Gateway Pipeline. The project's scope would include one terminal on the Pacific side of Panama and another on the Atlantic with a pipeline connecting the facilities. This would expand Energy Transfer's international operations into new markets while providing Panama the opportunity to establish itself as a distribution center of petroleum products to markets globally. This would give more flexibility to Panama and the Canal to better manage LNG and NGLs transits.

Proximity to the United States

The results from the pullback and unpredictability of American foreign policy will leave most of the world feeling flummoxed and trepidatious about what to do next. In fiscal year 2021, more than 72% of all tonnage handled by the Canal either originated or was destined for the United States. The Asian countries of China, Japan, and Korea were the next largest users of the Canal, followed by many countries across Latin America.[3] Being so close to the world's only superpower—historically, geographically, commercially, and culturally—reduces the risk to Panama from the global fallout of the Bretton Woods withdrawal.

Weaknesses Facing the Canal

Freshwater Usage and Management

One of the Canal's many impressive engineering accomplishments is how it uses so much of nature as its infrastructure. The lifeblood of the Canal is freshwater. It raises and lowers the ships in the locks. Water is what keeps Lake Gatun at levels where the ships can easily transit. Water makes the whole thing work.

Clearly aware of this, the management team of the Canal works hard to keep a reliable supply of freshwater readily available for Canal operations. However, this does not happen in a vacuum. Challenges around freshwater come from outside the

[3] Annual Report of ACP, 2021.

boundaries of the Canal Basin, that is, the two million-plus people who use the fresh water of the Canal's lakes and rivers for their daily needs. In addition, there are about 200,000 people who live within the Canal Basin and engage in productive, agricultural, and nonmetallic mining activities. From the Canal's lakes, in addition to what is consumed by ships in transit, about 500 million gallons are extracted each day for human consumption.

While the Canal and the government are fully aware of the challenge posed by freshwater insecurity—and have been taking reasonable actions to reduce the risk—it is not enough. Demand for water over the years has grown in such a way that the estimated level of consumption to be consumed in year 2025 was eclipsed way back in 2012. And, things are getting more acute. The source of the problem is twofold: poor water management and the population's attitude toward water.

Water management in Panama is poor. As someone who spends several months a year in the country, I can attest to how IDAAN, the public water company, is a badly run state-owned enterprise. Unannounced repairs and unexpected waterline shutdowns are a common source of jokes and complaints. The crumbling infrastructure regularly leads to several days without water in the home or business. However, it is deeper than just bad government management.

For some of this at least, we can blame the Americans. Overall, the United States did very little to help Panama during and after the construction of the Canal. It is true that the public health measures undertaken by the Americans significantly improved basic conditions on the Isthmus. However, none of the measures the Americans undertook were done to directly benefit the Panamanians. Instead, they were done to ensure completion of the work. Nonetheless, the near eradication of mosquitos across Panama—and the malaria and yellow fever they carry—is nothing to be dismissed. Cases of these scourges have been almost nonexistent in Panama for decades. Moreover, you can drink the water right out of the tap without any concern. Wastewater treatment approaches first-world levels.

Almost nowhere else in the tropical belt can you find a country with such strong public health *bona fides*. And herein lies some of the problem. Despite IDAAN's many shortcomings—and I am being kind—Panamanians over the decades have become accustomed to a predictable, clean, and cheap water supply. Water access remains predictable and clean because of much of the legacy of the American-built infrastructure. Cheap is because the Panamanian government subsidizes most of the water usage for homes and businesses. As a result, Panamanians have come to view nearly free water as a birthright. All this is re-enforced by the fact that Panama receives on average somewhere around 8–14 feet of rain—depending on the location—each year. That is a lot of moisture! This natural abundance of rainfall—combined with the incredibly low personal cost for usage and the entitlement mindset—finds Panamanians wasting huge quantities of water. A quick drive through any city center or its environs across Panama finds unattended water leaks from commercial buildings, homes, and even government offices that go on for weeks or more.

Although water has been known to be an issue for nearly two decades, the year 2019 was a wakeup call for many. Much of that year, it simply didn't rain much.

Gatun Lake and the Canal into which it feeds were way below any manageable levels for the ships making their transits. While the Canal was able to muddle through 2019, the repeat of a similar or worse situation could have a more serious effect. With Canal transits at record highs and the water management challenge in the country still not abated, another year or two of low rainfall could be devastating.

In Nature, change is the one constant; and, that includes the amount of rain that falls. Does this mean that the climate is inexorably changing and lower annual rainfall amounts will be the norm? No one knows. And, if they tell you they know, remember that they are only guessing.

What *is* known is that previous shortages have combined with Panama's poor water management system to create a situation where Canal operations have been negatively impacted. To its credit, the ACP has been extremely proactive in trying to resolve the water issues that it can control. Still, this has exposed a glaring weakness for the Canal.

Poor Supply Chain Infrastructure Quality Outside the Canal

A visit to the borders outside of the Canal on both coasts reveals a significant challenge to the overall operational effectiveness of Panama's integrated supply chain network. On the Atlantic side, the roads around the port of Cristobal and the Colon Free Zone are poor on their best day. Huge potholes fill entrances to all the neighboring support facilities. Trucks hauling cargo and containers regularly breakdown due to stress placed on their tires and chassis from the crumbling roads. Multi-mile-long traffic jams are regular occurrences due to the shortage of passable roads. Maintenance does take place, but it is almost always way short of what is really needed. The weather doesn't help. Colon's incessant tropical downpours happen year-round: easily washing away any repairs that might have been done. The same is true on the Pacific side. The traffic here is even worse. And, while there is not as much rain as the Atlantic side, the conditions of the roads can still be reduced. All this adds up to significant levels of inefficiency, unpredictability, and higher costs than there should be.

Anecdotally, none of this appears to be getting any better. In fact, over time, it seems like things have been getting worse. Various governmental agencies from the Ministry of Public Works to the provinces of Colon and Panama each have responsibility to maintain their portions of the public infrastructure. They have all come up short. This lack of focus can, in turn, impact the ability of the Canal and its users to fully leverage the benefits of Panama's prime location. A continued deficit of attention to the critical importance of the nation's infrastructure could leave a negative mark on the Canal's ability to deliver long-term value.

Moreover, despite Panama's stable government and the 5-year transitions that have marked its successful return to democracy, corruption is a potentially big challenge. This is not to say that all Panamanian institutions and leaders are corrupt.

They are not. Panama has a dynamic civil society where transparency is highly valued. Further, this not to say to say that Panama is some special place where the inputs and outputs of the human condition don't exist. They do—in all forms.

What matters here is that there are actors and organizations which—because of their proximity to the Canal's operations—might find opportunities to snake their way toward the billions of dollars of revenue the Canal generates each year. There are many non-Canal entities responsible for building and maintaining the infrastructure that connects the Canal to Panama's other transport modes. This includes actors from key ministries of the national government and the private contractors that do much of the actual work. Each of these could potentially influence the success of the Canal. Some of these parties could be mal-intentioned and might see the Canal as simply a gold mine to be exploited for their own gain.

Let's remember, Panama has been running the Canal for less than three decades. The expansion is just over 7 years old. The ACP and the country are going through the growing stages of ultimately defining what the Canal is and will it be for the nation. People and countries need time to figure things out. Time is the great thickener.

The potential for this kind of corruption is more subtle and yet just as corrosive over time. If this were allowed to transpire, it could turn the Canal into a den of political patronage, under-the-table dealing, and, in the end, something nobody except for a select few would ever want. For the Canal's leadership, continued vigilance that is rooted in robust transparency and public accountability is the only way to keep latent corrupting forces at bay.

Concerns About the Workforce of the Future

Another area that will require continuous attention of the ACP leadership is the development of the workforce of the future. Panama's children—the next generation of Canal's maintainers, welders, machine operators, mechanics, painters, et al.—have suffered immensely because of the lockdowns and other measures imposed to battle COVID-19. Most were "learning from home"—whatever that means—for 2 full years rather than engaging with their teachers, friends, and fellow students in person. Not surprising, like the rest of the world, Panama has seen a significant rise in the level of youth depression, teenage pregnancies, drug experimentation, and domestic abuse, which have all caused a precipitous decline in the overall well-being of her children. What the total impact of all this will remain unknown.

In summary, the Canal and the ACP that runs it possess a good number of significant strengths that work together to ensure its continued operational efficiency and profitability—including strong senior management, a high level of customer satisfaction, a loyal and productive workforce, overwhelming support from the Panamanian people, and the solid degree of political stability from the government of Panama.

There are areas of varying areas of weakness. At the top of the list is water management: both inside and outside of the Canal Basin. The continued growth of the Canal makes it more dependent—not less so—on outside parties for its sustainability. This can challenge the ability to maximize the entire package of integrated supply chain offerings that Panama provides. Also, the impact of the pandemic countermeasures on Panama's young people will need to be closely monitored in the years to come.

On balance, the current strengths of the Canal far outweigh the weaknesses, whether those of the present or the future. The nation of Panama and the ACP have shown tremendous resilience and flexibility over the past three decades. This will need to continue. It is clear the needed human, financial, and cultural resources exist within both the ACP and the country to handle any internal challenges. Nevertheless, the mere existence of the resources is not enough. The application is what will matter. Complacency must be proactively battled every day and on every front.

In Conclusion

A visitor to Panama today can easily observe the full integration of Panama with global commerce. A quick glance at the arrival and departure screens inside Tocumen International Airport confirms its position as *the* air transport hub for all Latin America. After entering the country, one can start with breakfast on the Causeway at the Pacific entrance to the Canal in Panama City. They would be instantly taken aback by the massive ships that approach to make the 50-mile trip north to the Atlantic or exit out to the "South Sea": all this in the shadow of the second largest skyline in the Western Hemisphere. Next, a 1-hour highway drive across the Continental Divide puts the traveler at Fort San Lorenzo, which guarded the Atlantic approach to the Chagres River for centuries. A short jog from there and the voyager can see up close both the original and new sets of Canal locks at Gatun: each working flawlessly to propel the 15% of all global trade that crosses the Isthmus each year. After a relaxing lunch at an outdoor bar-b-q, the afternoon passage through the rain forest on the Panama Railway returns the traveler to the Pacific, where they will enjoy—once again—the breathtaking skyline views along with the sunset and evening tropical breeze. There really is no other place on Earth where it is possible to see so much of our world in such a short period of time.

Panama's unique location allows it to punch far above its weight class. About the same size as the US state of South Carolina, the nation has been at the center of the expansion of global capitalism for large parts of the last 500 years. Presently, like the human heart, Panama works hard to ensure a continuous supply of oxygen and nutrients for the global economy.

Nonetheless, history is relentless. It doesn't sit idly by—and it despises complacency. The Canal was born long before anyone alive today was. It will be around long after we are all gone. The question is: what will the coming decades mean for the Canal and the global capitalist system it is part of?

The Canal Going Forward: The Global View

From this analysis, it is clear the vast majority of what will shape the future of the Canal lies beyond the control of both Panama and the ACP. The Panamanians have done an extraordinary job taking over the Canal and turning it into a world-class example of business professionalism and success. Nevertheless, significant changes in trade patterns and the global economy could very well impact the Canal's long-term viability.

History reminds us that in the sixteenth and seventeenth centuries, Panama was the hub of the New World. Then, because of factors outside of its control, Panama fell away into near obscurity. Today the country once again stands were it was: at the center of global commerce and transport. What happens in the broader space of world events will once again shape so much of the future of the Canal.

To be sure, the exploration of the Macro-trends in the previous chapter lays out a generally unflattering view of the future. Within the context of the COVID-19 pandemic, the horizon can look even more bleak. I am not a glass half-empty person. To borrow a phrase, I am rationally optimistic. However, what lies before us is fraught with challenges we have not had to deal with in nearly 80 years.

Principally, I am speaking of the American withdrawal from the same global system it created in 1944. Despite what the hype from the American "news" or politicians pronounce, safely ensconced in its continental "dominion from sea to sea," the United States will continue to enjoy the fruits of its seemingly endless bounty without major disruption or threat. Domestic shale energy is accelerating America's withdrawal from the Bretton Woods system it created and has supported.

As the rest of the world returns to "normal" without the guarantees of the American security blanket, ethnic and regional antipathies are flaring once again. Insecurity is breeding increased competition for critical supplies like energy and agricultural foodstuffs and rising military budgets. Driven by fears of scarcity—real or imagined—sometimes bordering on panic, nations are spending massively on their militaries and scouring the globe looking for resources to keep their populations warm, fed, and safe. Inevitably, war will follow.

For the ACP and the Canal, the unfolding chaos will have a major impact: some good, some not so good. Shale energy imports into a fracturing China, as well as the major Asian buyers (Japan, South Korea, India, in particular), will be in greater demand than ever before as more nations scramble to secure critical supplies. Every nation will be willing to pay whatever price is required to survive. The major importers will have an advantage because of their large holdings of dollars. As discussed at length, the Canal is well-positioned to handle American shale energy exports from the US East and Gulf coasts. In the coming years and beyond, this will be one of the Canal's fastest-growing, largest, and most profitable segments.

Agricultural imports will be much the same as energy imports. Famine will not be an option. Nations will do whatever it takes—and pay whatever price—to feed their people. Regarding agricultural exports, the United States ships most of its export product to Asia from the West Coast. Presently, the Canal is not well positioned for this market. However, and this warrants further exploration, if the continued inefficiencies, backlogs, delays, and price insecurities at America's West Coast ports linger on, another route via the Canal might become viable. That is, Gulf Coast or Southeast Atlantic ports using the Canal to get American agricultural products to Asia might make sense if the situation demanded. This is a stretch. Yet, in the turbulent world to come—where food insecurity is a major driver of national action—nothing is outside the realm of the possible. Also, increased agricultural exports from the East Coast of South America transiting the Canal may rise. As global food prices and demand skyrocket due to concerns over instability and insecurity, Brazil and Argentina will likely become even bigger export players.

On the container side of things, where manufacturing and consumer goods dominate, the Canal might face a flattening or even decline in that space. Shipments to and from Asia, particularly of containerized cargo, will likely be less—and maybe much less—than the recent past. The realigning of global supply chains around trends like regional reshoring, along with war or the real threat of war, make ocean shipping across the Pacific a much tougher proposition. The Chinese, Japanese, and Indian navies will be much more focused on getting the necessary energy and foodstuffs into their countries rather than protecting shipments of consumer goods. Further, the decline in the human population that is already underway will rewrite the rules when it comes to consumer demand.

We had a mere inkling of what kind of a world this would be like at the onset of the COVID-19 pandemic. Nations panicked and willingly violated all kinds of longstanding international and regional trade agreements to secure personal protective equipment (PPE) for their populations. Supplies such as face masks, plastic gloves, and ventilators went to the highest bidder. Niceties such as the European Union and the World Trade Organization never once figured into the calculus. It was a rush to protect me and mine at all costs. While this only lasted a couple of months, imagine a world where years of sustained global competition for the most important items in life such as plastic, ammonia, concrete, natural gas, rice, wheat, and steel persist. It is not merely hypothetical. It is a distinct possibility—and is what much of history looks like.

America Already in Retreat

As Russia reintroduced major war into Eurasia, first in 2008 with its invasion of Georgia, and later with the invasion of Ukraine in 2014, followed by the shoot down of a commercial airliner in 2016, the Americans under W. Bush and Obama did next to nothing. Trump was just as recalcitrant to act while in office.

At this writing, it appears the Biden Administration is not willing to risk American lives or significant treasure to ensure against the complete or partial takeover of Ukraine. Further, the rising Russian threat posed to other nations including Moldova, Poland, and the Baltics has Europe on high alert. Concerned about America's waning commitment, military spending on the Continent is suddenly way up, most notably in Germany.

In the Middle East, a cold war between Iran and Saudi Arabia is getting hot very quickly. Proxy wars in Syria, Iraq, and Yemen between the two regional powers have the real potential to become a direct confrontation. The arms race is building as both nations are spending billions to acquire the latest in offensive and defensive hardware. One or both nations eventually acquiring a nuclear capability are now a real and terrifying prospect.

In the South China Sea, concerns over Chinese territorial expansion and North Korea's nuclear program have Japan very worried about the veracity of America's guarantees of peace and stability in the region. It was no accident that the first foreign visitor to Trump Tower after the November 2016 election was Prime Minister Abe of Japan. Clearly not comfortable after his meeting with the President-Elect, Japan subsequently launched a massive military expansion at a level that has not been seen there since the early twentieth century. If it so desired, Japan could easily possess one of the world's largest nuclear arsenals in a matter of months. Japan's navy is already the second most formidable on Earth, only behind America's.

Further, like Japan, all the other nations of Asia, being so dependent on international shipping to transport their energy and food needs, are surging their own military capabilities to assure the continued flow of imports. China, facing unstoppable population decline along with internal political and economic crises, might finally recognize that its time in the sun is quickly fading. With the Americans less willing to act, the time to strike on Taiwan to expand China's defensive perimeter might be now.

Now firmly detached and increasingly disinterested, it is hard to imagine any popular support rising among the American people for their soldiers to fight and die over any of these places. This is not the Cold War where a national consensus about the Soviet Union and the threat of global communism held across most of the country until the 1980's—despite the frustrating results in Korea and Vietnam The complete failures in Iraq and Afghanistan have soured a large majority of the American population on the ideas of foreign intervention and nation building. Americans are no longer in the mood to go hunting enemies all over the planet.

Wars and rumors of wars among major nations are returning. Eventually, large powers will bang into each other as they scour the world for ever-scarcer resources and markets. Business costs will rise and friction will reign. People outside the United States intuitively know this and it scares them to death. This seems to be one of the primary reasons why so many world leaders hated Donald Trump. He gave a loud voice and a face to their worst fear: a world where America can no longer be counted on.

This does not mean, however, that Americans will refrain from exploring global business opportunities. Nor does it signify that American foreign policy will abandon all international pursuits. American corporations will still look to sell consumer goods, aircraft, arms and weapons, and energy to foreign markets where profits can be made. US foreign policy will advance these commercial interests, as it always has. This is good news for the Canal.

At the highest strategic level, America will continue to pursue a balance of power in Eurasia, thwarting any one nation from dominating the world's most critical land mass. Yet, what is already being reformulated is the level of intensity that has marked American global involvement since the creation of Bretton Woods. US energy ascendancy further fosters a level of American disengagement in global affairs that the nation—and the world—has not seen in decades. In short, the result is that American global activity will be less aggressive and less predictable. This combination is driving so much of the increase in non-American military spending. The world simply can't afford to sit idly by while the Americans figure things out, especially as American power is increasingly harnessed to work at home—rather than abroad. "America First" is rapidly becoming more and more the focus of US domestic politics on both sides of the aisl. And, the world viscerally knows it.

Anything Else?

Much of what has been presented here lies outside of the headlines from the daily news and talking heads. To best understand the world for what it is and might be, knowing history and recognizing the Macro-trends are what matter most. Consumed by the noise from our constant newsfeeds, we either don't know or have forgotten that the Canal was completed just over a century ago at the same time humanity entered the Carbon Era, that electrons and the atom were harnessed a mere nine decades ago, that many people made their first mobile call and sent their first text message in the late 1990s, and that building your network of "friends" and googling are exclusively twenty-first-century phenomena. Acknowledging history and the Macro-trends should humble us to our present condition as well as that of the future.

Concerning the future, all of the above is occurring in the midst of the COVID-19 pandemic. What if the pandemic flares up again—with several new waves of highly contagious variants which are more dangerous than what went before? What if, God forbid, a super variant emerges and throws all of us back to the starting line? In these circumstances, the fracturing of the current global order—driven by the Macro-trends and a renewed level of concern over the virus—would occur much quicker and more violently. The ability to react decisively in such a chaotic environment would be critical to long-term organizational survivability.

If, however, the pandemic fades quickly to an endemic phase, there will be opportunities to better manage the challenges of this new era. The Macro-trends are clear and some of their implications already identifiable. A shrinking human population, rising governmental insularity focused on protecting the home front, realigned supply chains driven to get closer to end users, rising global demand for energy, and so much more, as well as the implosion of China, all influenced by the American pullback, are taking humanity to a far different place than any of us will recognize. A substantially reduced virus would give decision-makers some breathing space to make needed adjustments.

To finish, the global economic system and the order that shaped so much of the postwar era—and for which the Canal was an active participant—is slipping away into history. It is being replaced by a much more uncertain, nationalistic, and dangerous world. What this all means for the prospects of the Canal of Panama and globalization is what this book has been about.

For the ACP and the Canal, the best thing they can do is to continue to focus on what is already done best: delivering high value to their clients and providing strong returns to the people of Panama. Ensuring that the Canal remains a global beacon of management excellence, adaptability, and high performance will go a long way to deal with the coming maelstrom.

GPSR Compliance
The European Union's (EU) General Product Safety Regulation (GPSR) is a set of rules that requires consumer products to be safe and our obligations to ensure this.

If you have any concerns about our products, you can contact us on

ProductSafety@springernature.com

In case Publisher is established outside the EU, the EU authorized representative is:

Springer Nature Customer Service Center GmbH
Europaplatz 3
69115 Heidelberg, Germany

www.ingramcontent.com/pod-product-compliance
Lightning Source LLC
Chambersburg PA
CBHW062119180525
26896CB00003B/48
* 9 7 8 3 0 3 1 0 5 1 5 1 7 *